AMERICAN STRUGGLE
TEENS RESPOND TO JACOB LAWRENCE

AMERICAN STRUGGLE:
TEENS RESPOND TO JACOB LAWRENCE

Published by Six Foot Press
Coert Voorhees, President
Chul R. Kim, Publisher

in association with
Peabody Essex Museum, Salem, Massachusetts

Published on the occasion of the exhibition
Jacob Lawrence: The American Struggle,
organized by the Peabody Essex Museum

Exhibition Itinerary

Peabody Essex Museum
January 18–April 26, 2020

The Metropolitan Museum of Art, New York
June 2–September 7, 2020

Birmingham Museum of Art, Birmingham, Alabama
October 17, 2020–January 10, 2021

Seattle Art Museum, Seattle
February 25–May 31, 2021

The Phillips Collection, Washington, DC
June 26–September 19, 2021

NATIONAL ENDOWMENT for the ARTS
arts.gov

The exhibition was supported in part by the National
Endowment for the Arts. Carolyn and Peter S. Lynch and
The Lynch Foundation, Jennifer and Andrew Borggaard,
and Kate and Ford O'Neil provided generous support.
We also recognize the generosity of the East India Marine
Associates of the Peabody Essex Museum.

First edition 2020
© 2020 Six Foot Press

Preface © 2019 Barbara Earl Thomas
Lawrence panel texts © 2019 Peabody Essex Museum
Teen texts are copyrighted in the name of each writer

All works by Jacob Lawrence © 2020 The Jacob and
Gwendolyn Knight Lawrence Foundation,
Seattle/Artist Rights Society (ARS), New York

Struggle: From the History of the American People series:
Panels 1–3, 5–8, 12–13, 17–18, 21–25: Photo by
Bob Packert/PEM
Panels 4, 26, 27: Photo by Seattle Art Museum
Panel 9: Photo by Greg Staley
Panel 10: Photo by The Metropolitan Museum of Art
Panels 11, 30: Photo by Stanford University
Panels 14, 28, 29: Courtesy of Lucia | Marquand
Panel 15: Photo by Harvard Art Museums
Panel 19: Photo by Stephen Petegorsky

Edited by Chul R. Kim
Designed by Bright Sky Publishing
Printed by Four Colour Printing Group, Louisville, KY
This book is typeset in Avenir® Next by Linotype

Library of Congress Cataloguing-in-Publication data
available from the publisher

Distributed throughout the world
by Ingram Publisher Services
www.ingrambook.com

Printed in the United States

Cover: Panel 1 (detail), 1955. Collection of Harvey
and Harvey-Ann Ross

AMERICAN STRUGGLE
TEENS RESPOND TO JACOB LAWRENCE

Edited by Chul R. Kim

Writing by teens working with

Peabody Essex Museum / The Metropolitan Museum of Art
Schomburg Center for Research in Black Culture
The Studio Museum in Harlem / Birmingham Museum of Art
Seattle Art Museum / The Phillips Collection
Thurgood Marshall Academy
Boston Community Leadership Academy

With contributions by Austen Barron Bailly, Lydia Gordon,
Barbara Earl Thomas, and Elizabeth Hutton Turner

Published in association with the
Peabody Essex Museum, Salem, Massachusetts
on the occasion of the exhibition
Jacob Lawrence: The American Struggle

SIXFOOTPRESS
Houston

CONTENTS

Panel 5 (detail), 1955. Collection of Harvey and Harvey-Ann Ross

PREFACE
TENDER BEAUTY, WOUNDED HOPE
Barbara Earl Thomas

When I met Jacob Lawrence in the mid-1970s, our country still smoldering from the civil rights struggle, he was already an elder artist-statesman who was at times criticized for not being openly strident enough in his political views. When asked about this, he replied,

"Everything I have to say is in my paintings." And he was indeed a master storyteller, a bellwether, fluent, sublime. This series is his truth, evidenced; it magnifies an epic through line that contemplates the question: When have we not been in struggle? Swords crossed, knives drawn, lives on the line; the deeply jewel-rich but somber palette matches the gravity of the event. The American Revolution is the genesis, but it also becomes the human struggle made universal. Lawrence was already a master in 1954, and his exquisite compositions and controlled use of color anchor the work in concert with the diagonal underpinnings that create high-pitched emotion. Muskets and knives crisscross to move the eye around the picture plane, in time to the battle's drumbeat. These tightly composed dramas are stage front, set in shallow landscapes. Hear the thud as metal strikes flesh and bone; feel the desperation of bodies locked in combat. In Lawrence's hands, would-be journalism is transformed to reveal the frailty of our dreams. "For freedom we want and will have," he quotes in panel 27, as he ties and unties the knot of our longing. He delivers each brushstroke saturated in the pigment of tender beauty and wounded hope.

NOTE FROM THE EDITOR
Chul R. Kim

Photo: U.S. Coast Guard

The paintings which I propose to do will depict the struggles of a people to create a nation and their attempt to build a democracy. . . . I therefore hope that these paintings when completed will serve in some small way to further enlighten those who come in contact with them of the struggles, contributions, and ingenuity of the American people. —Jacob Lawrence, 1954

Jacob Lawrence (1917-2000) was one of the most important American artists of the twentieth century. In his painting series *Struggle: From the History of the American People* (1954-56), he not only revived the struggles of America's founding fathers, but also viewed early American history from the perspective of the marginalized. His landmark series has never been more important than in today's political climate, especially to young Americans.

Teenagers, most of whom participate in educational programs run by the museums hosting the *Jacob Lawrence: The American Struggle* exhibition, were invited to reinterpret Lawrence's series through their own lived experiences. In free and structured verse, historical analysis, memoir, political commentary, and more, they showed us how Jacob Lawrence and his art remain crucial and fresh in this new millennium. We present a curated selection of their writings here, with gratitude for their perceptiveness and wisdom.

CHAPTER ONE

STRUGGLE FOR FREEDOM

Trécii Cheeseboro (Schomburg Center for Research in Black Culture)

A Few Examples of Modern-day Freedom

Response to Panel 5, *We have no property! We have no wives! No children! We have no city! No country! –petition of many slaves, 1773*

A few examples of modern-day freedom are equal-paying jobs, equal education, justice for the living, justice for the lost, and an opportunity at life.

Some cases of modern-day slavery are poverty, child slavery, debt bondage, human and sex trafficking, and forced labor.

"We have no property!…"
Gentrification and displacement are overtaking black and brown communities.

Pushing those who reside out of homes where families were born and raised.
Out of homes that were passed on from generations.
Out of homes with potentially nowhere to go because the supremes felt the need to renovate and improve these communities.
These communities hold affordable housing.
This painting embodies the image of minorities fighting financial issues, displacement, and homelessness.

"We have no wives! No children!…"
The souls of black men, black women, black children are being stripped away by those in uniform with badges.
By those in masks.
Murdered with their hands behind their heads.
Murdered by façades.
Murdered possessing no weapon.
Imprisoned with no evidence.
Black men, on average, are being sentenced nearly 20% longer than white men for the same crime.
Young boys are being incarcerated, charged as adults.
These boys are often wrongfully convicted, which is a perfect example of this corrupt system robbing them of their lives.
These paintings display women, men, boys, girls, mothers, fathers, children battling for justice.

Felix Holbrook, Peter Bestes, Sambo Freeman, and Chester Joie were depicted requesting freedom from the government.
These four men could be linked to The Exonerated Five (The Central Park 5), who were wrongfully accused and convicted of crimes.

These crimes include assault, robbery, riot, rape, sexual abuse, and attempted murder.
See, these five men, till this day, are still fighting for their freedom.
Fighting against the blind eyes that insist on portraying them as animals instead of what they were, children.
Trump is a demagogue who throws salt into their wounds by calling for the death penalty for the innocent black and brown community, including the youth.
It goes to show that not a lot has changed since the 1700s around these issues.

Sure, Yusef Salaam, Kevin Richardson, Antron McCray, Korey Wise, and Raymond Santana are no longer imprisoned.
Sure, their stories are being told.
Sure, they received millions of dollars.
Sure, they have taken on normal lives, gotten married, started families, but they will forever be mentally enslaved.

Kevin Deleon
(Schomburg Center for Research in Black Culture)

Me!

Response to Panel 5, *"We have no property! We have no wives! No children! We have no city! No country!"* *–petition of many slaves, 1773*

But I'm here! I may not have anything, anything that shows my worth, my stature, my strength as a human being, but I have myself! I'm here for myself, for my freedom. I may not have the power, the authority, or the respect to stand here, but I have myself. With myself, with ME, I will break through these fences, through this gate, and dance through the open field you once owned.

"Felix," the author of the petition to which this panel's inscription refers, is a beacon of self-liberation and the willingness to fight back. "Felix" is not just a person, but also an entity that broadens the idea of what the fight for liberation is. It is as Jacob Lawrence saw with the rise of the civil rights movement: there was no one way of gaining the freedom African Americans sought. Martin Luther King, Jr., and Malcolm X come to mind as examples of different ideas clashing head to head. In his painting, Lawrence shows this division through violence that fights for the same cause. The complexion of the groups in the painting is something to be highlighted, as differences between them are far in between. Two distinct methods, ideas, ideologies are clashing to reach the same goal. "Felix" is represented on both sides. Both groups strive for freedom, but their method of achieving it differs, causing a conflict.

Aminata Dosso (Metropolitan Museum of Art)

Middle School

Response to Panel 5, *We have no property! We have no wives! No children! We have no city! No country! –petition of many slaves, 1773*

"She's only being mean to me because that's how friends joke," I thought to myself. I believed no one wanted to be friends with me, all throughout middle school. I was holding on to a friend group that was nothing but toxic to me. How was I supposed to know, I mean I never had any other friends. I'd rather have friends that made me feel like shit than none at all. Everyone made it seem like being by yourself was the worst-case scenario, so of course I didn't want to be the outcast. When you're in middle school, being by yourself means that you aren't accepted or liked. So I was less afraid of being alone and more afraid of what people were thinking of my being alone.

When I started eighth grade, it became evident to me that if I didn't stand up for myself I would be stuck in a "friendship" where I gained no happiness. But I hadn't developed the strength that I needed to do so. When I looked at panel 5, I saw black men fighting against the very thing that seemed to be holding them up; this reminded me of how I thought that ending this friendship would be like letting go of the only thing keeping me from being invisible and irrelevant in anyone's life.

Once I started high school last year, I let go. It was hard in the beginning because I had to stop meeting up with those toxic friends before school, sitting with them during lunch, and hanging out with them after school. They started to ask me questions like "Are you too bougie to hang out with us now?" and "Do you think you're better than us or something?" These questions were pretty rhetorical. The point of them was not to get an actual answer from me but to cut ties officially. It was so easy for these people to let go of me, while I was stuck in the past, reliving our past moments over and over.

I was bullied in middle school, as many people are, and these "friends" gave me more a sense of protection than of companionship. Ending the friendship would mean putting my shield down and being open to any and all attacks. But I did it anyway. I decided that if I didn't end the friendship sooner, the end would still eventually come, and I wanted to live my high school years without the burden of being someone I'm not. What gave me the strength was that I had a friend outside this toxic group, and whenever I hung out with her, I was happy. I was actually excited to see her; I always dreaded being around the other group. I could never fully be myself without feeling like they were judging me, either behind my back or to my face. In the *Struggle* series, Jacob Lawrence depicts struggle in various ways, but for panel 5, I saw it in a way that can be overcome. Such as this obstacle in my life: I overcame it and I learned from it.

Jada Epps
(Phillips Collection/Thurgood Marshall Academy)

The Aftermath

Response to Panel 16, *There are combustibles in every State, which a spark might set fire to. —Washington, 26 December 1786*

According to the Declaration of Independence, "Whenever any form of government becomes destructive of these ends, it is the right of the people to alter or to abolish it." The War of Independence, they called it. But no one discussed what would happen afterwards.

After bodies were filled with bullets, husbands and fathers gone forever, wives left to raise children on their own, they were "free." No one warned about the aftermath. Families left impoverished. Veterans forever reminded of the fight that let them "free." Taxes and penalties for a state that wanted them to no longer be controlled. Sound familiar? The fight for *freedom*.

My ancestors fought for their freedom with their scarred backs, blackened skin, and silent wounds that told stories of the unforgivable horrors they suffered. The Civil War, they called it. Bloodshed, children and men. Never returning home. *A fight for freedom, they called it.*

My black men, gunned down, treated like dogs, discarded like trash. A fight for equality, we call it.

So when you ask, "How do you see struggle in this painting?" I see a corrupt government. A president holding people in camps. I see powerful people doing nothing to change our society.

I don't see *freedom. I still see us FIGHTING.*

Jillian Peprah-Frimpong (Schomburg Center for Research in Black Culture)

Vessels Containing Anxious Men

Response to Panel 10, *We crossed the River at McKonkey's Ferry 9 miles above Trenton…the night was excessively severe…which the men bore without the least murmur… —Tench Tilghman, 27 December 1776*

Vessels containing anxious men violently sway on a bed of tumultuous waves. Trapped in a storm, George Washington and his men are left to face the currents and winds of the unknown. The boats are rusted and beaten from months of drifting in choppy waters. Frail green, yellow, and white tents poke out from each boat in a futile attempt to protect the disheveled Continental Army from the elements. Silver-headed spears stick out from the boats erratically as if in duel with the weather.

Inscribed on the back of the painting are the words of Washington's extremely devoted aide-de-camp, Tench Tilghman: "severe." At a time of low morale for the colonial public during the Revolutionary War, Washington believed spirits could be boosted if he and his troops could cross the Delaware River and defeat the Hessians. United with his men in their desire for legitimacy and liberation, Washington led them across the river and made it to an isolated area. This strategy proved victorious for the American colonists yearning for freedom from Great Britain.

This painting evokes a sense of helplessness, which stems from the experience of struggle, while the men are subject to the uncertain whims of nature. If we are placed in the direction of the unknown, we enter a fight-or-flight state of mind, which can result in protection in the short term but agony in the long term. In this case, the army enters fight mode in order to resuscitate a chance of gaining freedom. The men sit stone-faced underneath their tents and rain shields, floating along the rippling water.

In today's context, this painting can be understood as the universal struggle to express fear, worry, and anxiety, which stems from a fear of being judged. The true struggle depicted is the expression of emotions. Although the soldiers probably questioned their fate after Washington ordered them to cross the Delaware, they remained stoic about their conditions. This fight wasn't about them, their well-being and emotions, it was about independence and the future of the American colonists. However, this compromise between the greater good of the nation and emotions of individuals must have left them emotionally barren.

Not only did the troops question what was to be their fate, whether they would make it out alive in the end, but they must have questioned the significance of their crossing in the bigger picture of the Revolutionary War. Was this sacrifice worth the liberation? How would they implement their newfound ideals of democracy and freedom? And most important, with the monarch no longer ruling, who would have power, and who would be subject to that power? Since then, one thing that hasn't changed generally is the human desire for dominance. Our emotions are sacrificed for the retention of power.

Braden Kislin
(The Leffell School)

Freedom Is a Struggle

Response to Panel 5, *We have no property! We have no wives! No children! We have no city! No country! –petition of many slaves, 1773*

Four thousand years ago, the Jewish people were slaves of the Pharaoh in Egypt, forced to till the fields and build the pyramids, without freedom. In the Torah, a sacred Jewish text, God tells the Pharaoh, through Moses, of the wickedness of slavery and demands, "Let my people go!" The Pharaoh is unmoved, even after nine serious plagues are visited upon the Egyptians. Only after the tenth, the killing of all firstborn Egyptian males, does he relent. But as the Jews are fleeing across the desert, the Pharaoh changes his mind and has his chariots chase them—only to see his soldiers drown in the Red Sea as the Jews miraculously escape.

It is not easy to gain one's freedom; it requires determination, persistence, bravery, and often violence. In the United States, it took the Civil War and 600,000 deaths to finally end slavery. And even then, with Jim Crow laws, sharecropping, and segregation, the liberated slaves and their descendants were separate but not equal. In 1954, when Jacob Lawrence started painting the *Struggle* series, many African-American citizens had their voting rights suppressed, and their children were forced to attend segregated schools. But times were changing, and by the 1960s, legislation advanced civil rights, including voting rights. Panel 5 in the *Struggle* series shows slaves fighting with their masters to obtain their freedom. As a petition submitted by slaves in Massachusetts in 1773 stated, "We have no property! We have no wives! No children! We have no city! No country!" The broken chain in the painting signifies that no human should be a slave, but also that one must fight for one's freedom. It represents not only individual slaves but the collective effort of the country to overcome this "original sin." It took many fights and thousands of casualties for African Americans to gain their freedom. The Declaration of Independence states, "We hold these truths to be self-evident, that all men are created equal, that they are endowed by their Creator with certain unalienable rights, that among these are life, liberty, and the pursuit of happiness." It has taken a very long time, but in 2019, the United States continues to struggle with freedom, striving for Jacob Lawrence's dream.

Jamiah Lewis
(Phillips Collection/Thurgood Marshall Academy)

Why Choose Violence?

Response to Panel 25, *I cannot speak sufficiently in praise of the firmness and deliberation with which my whole line received their approach…* —Andrew Jackson, New Orleans, 1815

Bloodshed. Multiple weapons. A fallen ladder. All the men in red are dead. These were my observations when looking at panel 25. Our nation has a reputation of bloodshed due to lack of communication. Because of the failure to convey word that the Treaty of Ghent, ending the War of 1812, had been drawn up and signed, the Americans and the British fought the Battle of New Orleans, as painted here. Jacob Lawrence's painting symbolizes two very important ongoing problems, racial oppression and lack of communication.

As I sit here, thoughts flowing onto paper, a question lingers in my mind: Why? What was the initial conflict? Couldn't an attempt at comprehension and exchange have rectified the issue? If not, why choose violence?

These are the same questions I ask when I hear gunshots, when I hear about another situation of police brutality, when I hear there is still foreign conflict that's been going on the past sixteen years of my life. Then I think of the purpose of the Declaration of Independence when my people are still not free. What was the American victory for in this painting? In 1815, the ladder—the goal—was colonization and control of America by Britain; today the ladder is controlled by white supremacists. The ladder in the painting might be down for America, but contrary to what the Declaration of Independence states about freedom, it isn't down for today's America.

Sunah Nash (Schomburg Center for Research in Black Culture)

___

Let's Not Forget

___

General response

Let's not forget
All the blood spilled
All the minds scarred
All the bodies sacrificed
To this future

Tied up in bows made of this past
Disguised as beautiful
Tethered to the subconscious minds of
Unborn children
And propelled into tomorrow
With enough ammunition
To fuel a rocket

Let's not forget
All those who will pay for this pain
It will only breed more pain
Because that is what pain does
It is a blackberry stain seeped
All the way through
And everybody knows those don't come out
You can cover them up
But that won't lift them
You can buy a new shirt
But that won't fix the old one
The blemish is still there
Surely as we are

Do not attempt to bury it
Acknowledge the ugliness
It may be ugly
But it is not meaningless
Because no one tries to bury
Meaningless things
Anyway

You cannot walk through life
Pretending we cannot feel the truth
Under the ground
Through the soles of our feet
Some of us remember, because some of us
Were never given the chance to forget
You cannot make these marks normal
They will always be unusual
You will never convince this land that
Your filth is only soil
That your dirt is only earth
That your waste is really manure
We know it is not
We have fertilized ourselves
With the remains of our own fallen
Because nothing sustainable has ever grown
From the lies you have told us

Madison Stephenson (Schomburg Center for Research in Black Culture)

The Fight of the Enslaved and Resistance Toward Their Freedom

---

Response to Panel 5, *We have no property! We have no wives! No children! We have no city! No country! —petition of many slaves, 1773*

In panel 5 of his *Struggle* series, Jacob Lawrence expresses the fight of the enslaved and resistance toward their freedom. The title quotes from a petition of enslaved blacks, brought by force to the Americas, who cried out the injustices of their reality. Lawrence Illustrates this by painting enslaved black people on the right of the painting, attacking a wall with spears. The wall symbolizes all things preventing freedom—the government, white slave owners, and even peaceful protest. This wall must be broken down in order for the goals of the enslaved to be met; this is why Lawrence only paints the wall as being pierced. The spears are shown piercing the wall but the slaves are depicted as lifeless, their eyes are dark, and blood drips from their bodies. The blood evokes the toll of the labor they were made to carry out and the harsh conditions in which they lived. It represents the physical and emotional pain of the slaves. But on the other side of the wall, Lawrence shows a black man resisting violent forms of protest.

With injustice toward the black community continuing today, opposing routes to justice still exist. In exhibition curator Austen Barron Bailly's analysis, Lawrence's paintings foreshadowed the events of the civil rights movement. The notion of violent versus peaceful protest is still debated today, as seen at Black Lives Matter protests and gun-control marches; it is common to see people whose goals align but whose approaches differ. In Lawrence's painting, violent and peaceful protest face each other, are pinned against each other—when in actuality they are on the same team.

CHAPTER TWO

STRUGGLE TO BELONG

Sam Ahn (Metropolitan Museum of Art)

A Poem for Umma, My Mother

Response to Panel 28, *Immigrants admitted from all countries: 1820 to 1840—115,773*

Umma and I spend a lot of time in
cars together.
My mother, who rode the bus with infant in
one hand and toddler's fist in the other,
proudly declares that she
     knows the ins and outs and all the
          secret roads that my father was
          too stubborn to ever know about.
"Korean mothers are surprised when I
tell them that I can drive you to school,
you know." She
         takes out her clip-on shades,
puts them on her glasses,
     grins, asks how she looks. We laugh,
she asks me whether I would like a pair, and I
             say no.
She retreats and
     puts her shades
      away.

She tells me, "In high school, I had to recite
the school's pledge in front of the
whole student body. A boy had always been
president, but I
changed that."
She has told me this story before,
but she says it anyway.
She tells me, it does not matter if you hear it
again if you do not listen.

Umma can speak in her mother tongue for
an hour without taking a breath,
but a mention of my friend's strange names
      stone her tongue until it barely moves,
      until it
            lies on the floor frail and bruised.
She tells me, "I do not understand
why you are afraid to lead the world.
Why you will not listen to
      what I tell you to do." And I
         yell, my throat a perfectly
         horrible melting pot of
my father and mother's years of screaming
and empty words, my throat that only
         gets stronger the more I yell.
My mother says, "I've given you nothing
      but love, I've
            given you nothing but all
      of myself."
And soon we are tired of the thunder, of
throwing stones and hitting
exactly on target, and we
      keep driving.

My umma tells me about her summer plans.
"While you are away at camp and your
father is working,

I will go to Los Angeles.
I will raise your baby nephew while
Hyung and Hyungsoo are working. I do not
want a stranger to raise him." She
      smiles, grips the steering wheel,
ready to leave, ready to be
under a new sun, to
bathe her wrinkles and let her calluses
            fade away.
Two days later, my brother calls home.
You cannot come, the stranger says.
You give my wife a headache,
and she doesn't like you.
She has not liked you from the
beginning, Umma.
You are the reason we fight.
My mother says,
"Why have I lost my son to another woman?
Why are you listening to her?
Did you even put up a fight?"

My umma is easy to let rain fall from her eyes
but unable
to strike lightning at her world.
"In Korea, children respect their parents.
They listen and
      are kind, loving.
What has my life become?"

My umma looks to her right to an empty
passenger seat.
She puts on her clip-on shades on her glasses,
      steps on the gas,
         speeding
away toward an
      unforgiving sun.

Saudia Campbell (Phillips Collection/Thurgood Marshall Academy)

Fight

Response to Panel 27, *…for freedom we want and will have, for we have served this cruel land long enuff… –a Georgia slave, 1810*

All we do is fight
We fight for our lives we fight for our rights
We fight for change because we are tired of
Things staying the same
Nat Turner was fed up with the ways
Blacks were being treated
He fought and killed the slave masters
Until at last he was defeated
They were scared of a man with a pen
They act like David Walker's words were a sin
He was just a man using his words
As a way to enlighten
They were so scared that they
Became frightened
David Walker taught blacks to keep
Their heads up and fight
But they tried to keep his words out of sight
As time went along things still were the same
So that's why people like Malcolm X had
To rise and fight to change the game
Martin Luther King, Jr., was nothing
Like Malcolm

He was peaceful and wanted to wait to see
The outcome
Claudette Colvin fought for the right
To sit in the front of the bus
She didn't move out of her seat and that
Ended up helping us
We fought for the right to vote
We fought so that people wouldn't take
Our marches as a joke
You would think by the 2000s things
Would change
Blacks had new rights but still had to fight
What an outrage
We are suffering from gun violence
But we know we can't stay silent
We shout "Black Lives Matter"
Because that shows we are fighters
We fight to be heard and not just seen
We fight for all to know that we are
Human beings
The medical fields have lined us up as
Guinea pigs at testing sites
Lord knows that the black death toll is high
They act like we have no rights
We fight for those who suffered in the
Tuskegee study of untreated syphilis in
Negro males
Who were too misinformed to consent
The trade-off was free medical exams
Food, and burial assistance, how is that decent
I have a dream that everyone will be equal
But I guess we will find out in the sequel

Yasmine Chokrane (Metropolitan Museum of Art)

The Common Struggle

Response to Panel 23, ...*if we fail, let us fail like men and expire together in one common struggle...*
—Henry Clay, 1813

To be a first-generation American is to learn to sympathize with a pendulum.

It's continuously oscillating between two extremes, resting at the top of two opposing sides and scrambling to meet the center.

To be a first-generation American is learning to navigate Dante's Ante-Inferno.

The Ante-Inferno, the special place in hell where those who are neither good nor bad march to follow a blank banner. It's their punishment for failing to live without distinction, and it's the first-generation American's struggle in failing to pick a "side."

To be a first-generation American is to walk every day in Janus's shoes.

The Roman god of duality and transitions is often depicted with two faces: one looking to the past, one looking to the future, and neither looking to the other. It's two ideals constantly contradicting, it's opposites failing to attract, and it's a struggle internalized.

It's our struggle internalized.

Because being a first-generation teenage American, as my identity comes into fruition and my singular personality forms, I've found just a hodgepodge of beliefs and ideas, where the traditional Islamic ideals of my immigrant parents lie and the Western values of the USA overlap.

I'm a first-generation American because I am the daughter of immigrants and was born in America. Both my parents come from Morocco. I was born in New York City, but part of me also comes from Morocco, because I believe in Aristotle's idea of tabula rasa, a blank slate until otherwise imprinted on. And on me lie different types of ink, handwriting, as well as verses of the Qur'an written in classical Arabic, but also the First Amendment of our Bill of Rights.

Being a first-generation American, I've learned to manage fasting during exam season, to reconcile my religious turmoil with the understanding that I need energy in order to do well.

Being a first-generation American, I've learned to maintain some of those Islamic ideals in a mostly secular nation, to view religion as a guiding hand and science as my two legs: religion shows me where to go, science ensures my way to get there.

Because being a first-generation American, I've learned to navigate the "middle," just as the Americans did in the Battle of Lake Erie, where they defeated the British from reaching the middle of the United States, in the turning point of the War of 1812.

But being an American, I've learned to reject the idea of an American identity, and instead to recognize all the cultures and people imprinted on the terrain of the Adirondack Mountains, on the treacherous rocks of the Grand Canyon, on the waters of Lake Erie, as Americans. We exist in multiplicities, and for those whose families have been here for generations, it's a fact they've learned to accept.

For me, it's a fact I find comfort in and it has made the struggle that much easier to manage.

Amber Cruz
(Studio Museum in Harlem)

A Painting Showing Loss

Response to Panel 23, *...if we fail,
let us fail like men, and expire together
in one common struggle...*
—Henry Clay, 1813

When looking at the *Struggle* series, I was overwhelmed by how many bold colors demanded my complete attention as they moved in sharp lines across the paintings. This is likely why my eyes settled on the piece I have decided to discuss. The white, gray, and deep navy blue that make up the majority of panel 23 soothed my eyes. The quotation used in the title intrigued me as well.

I remember reading those words in my eleventh-grade AP United States history class when we studied the War of 1812. I remember learning about how much Americans did not like "Mr. Madison's War," and that Henry Clay was among those few who were excited, the War Hawks. With this quotation in mind, the fairly abstract image I saw began to make more sense to me. The jagged lines cutting into smoothed, curved white boxes were torn sails; the soft rounded gray masses were clouds; and the deep navy that reminded me of my uniform pants was a dark stormy sky. I did not even need to look at the central figure to see that this was a painting showing loss, more specifically American loss, which seems to be either glorified so as not to focus on horror or forgotten in order to prevent shame. The central figure is still powerful, a man, probably a sailor, an American, stabbed in the eye by an invisible assailant, and dropping his sword, the weapon with which he probably fought for his freedom until his dying breath.

I wonder if that is what Lawrence was showing in the image. How, much as the sailor in his painting, people of color will always fight for their freedoms as humans and Americans until their last breath. That is my own personal take, which is difficult not to have when growing up in today's twenty-four-hour news cycle. Most of what I hear concerns people having their rights, freedoms, and even lives taken from them. All because someone thought they did not deserve these human rights, as they did not share the same race, ethnicity, sexuality, gender, religion, education, class, physical ability, mental ability, or some combination. If there were a box next to each term listed, I would check about half the boxes. I am lucky to live where I live, though, where the diverse crowd allows anyone to feel welcome. There are those who are not so lucky, and I think about them, in places not nearly as welcoming. Still, they rise. In protests, rallies, and parades, they rise to proudly say they exist, they deserve to exist, and they deserve their rights, and they join hands to say they will fight for their beliefs until their last breath.

Savannah Milton (Schomburg Center for Research in Black Culture)

The Motif of Struggle

Response to Panel 28, *Immigrants admitted from all countries: 1820 to 1840–115,773*

The piece that spoke to me the most from the *Struggle* series is panel 28. It shows different stories of why immigrants came to America, and what they brought with them. The elongated, droopy shapes of the bodies give the painting a somber look. The panel emphasizes the motif of struggle and shows the pain associated with leaving home for a foreign country. The painting also reminds those whose ancestors were enslaved that tracing their history is hard, maybe impossible, because their ancestors were regarded as property and not humans.

This touched me because I have felt the pain of not knowing where my family comes from. It made me sad when I heard others proudly talk about their families' origins. I couldn't do the same because I knew nothing. I had asked my family for information, especially my grandmother, but she didn't even remember where her mother was born. This inspired me to take up the quest of learning about my family history.

I started by looking online for census records and came across familysearch.com. It had free access to U.S. Censuses since 1870, so I searched for my great-grandmother Mary Cecelia Reed. At first I was extremely frustrated because I couldn't find the right person; Mary Cecelia seemed to be a very popular name in the period when my great-grandmother was born, so I had to sift through a lot of people before I could find her. Thirty minutes into my search, I found the marriage license for her wedding with my great-grandfather James Edward Herbert; she was eighteen. Twenty minutes later, I found her again, with her mother, father, siblings, husband, and daughter in the 1940 Census. I knew it was my great-grandmother, because her daughter, who is still alive today and whom I know, was in it with her correct birthdate.

I was so happy to find them, and immediately showed my grandmother, my great-grandmother's third daughter. She was happy, too: she finally knew more about her mother, something she'd always dreamed of. I was proud of myself for finding this information, but I didn't stop there. There was still a lot of family I didn't know. Next, I searched for my great-great-grandmother. It was a lot harder with her because I had only her name, but after two days of on-and-off searching, I found her, too.

Over the next five months, I slowly found family members from as far back as 1820. That is all I've discovered thus far, but I hope to find more. My plan now is to verify the information I've found online with other members of my family and then find a way to preserve it so that the people after me won't struggle like I did. They'll be able to tell people proudly who they are and where they're from. That is the one thing I want to leave behind when I die, so that people know that my family existed and that their lives were important.

Brianna Santiago (Boston Community Leadership Academy)

———

The Struggle of Immigration

———

Response to panel 30, *Old America seems to be breaking up and moving Westward . . .* —an English immigrant, 1817

Jacob Lawrence tells the story of the African American journey through the art of painting. He created this thirty-panel series in which each work tells a different story but is connected to the struggles many encounter in life. Lawrence himself faced major struggles, from being in foster care because of the divorce of his parents to dropping out of school at sixteen to work. But through it all, he never stopped painting, no matter the obstacles he faced, and I admire him so much for that.

As the granddaughter of immigrants from Puerto Rico, I am able to relate to panel 30 the most. I find it important to learn about the journey my grandparents took and the challenges they faced. I also feel connected to our homeland and the family we still have there. In 2017, Hurricane Maria damaged the island and left it without electricity, cutting off all communication to families and loved ones. I remembered being so scared because we went weeks without hearing from aunts, uncles, and cousins who were stranded. Not knowing if they were okay or if they were hurt frightened me beyond words.

In panel 30, two oxen cross a river while pulling a wagon, showing how immigrants traveled by foot to reach their destination. The oxen carried all of their supplies and belongings. Sometimes, if people were sick or injured, they were allowed to sit on the wagon, which only added more weight for the oxen to pull. The journey itself caused pain and exhaustion to both the people and the oxen, but no matter how much suffering they felt, they kept on moving, using all the strength they had. To me, this painting shows immigrants fighting through pain, sadness, stress, and challenges, knowing that soon enough they would be in a better place with their family. I feel sad knowing that many immigrants died on long journeys looking for a place where they could live safely, but I also imagine the joy they felt when they crossed the border into their future.

To this day, immigrants from all over the world come to America searching for happiness, safety, job opportunities, and to join their families. I understand their motivations—finding ways to provide for their families and working hard to prove they are worth something. It is important that their stories are being read in books and newspapers and studied in school so that immigrants and their children know that they are not alone.

L'hussen De Kolia Touré (Schomburg Center for Research in Black Culture)

My Representation of Manliness

Response to Panel 14, *Peace*

Hauling my body over to Planet Fitness, I tremble at the thought that someone will see me for the interloper that I am. To distract myself, I play a Nicki Minaj song that fills my hips with a boisterous energy. A peacock gait consumes me. I suddenly hear, "He even look like a faggot. Don't he?" I pause the song to observe the antagonist's scornful visage fully. I recall that he works at the car wash that my mother goes to regularly, though his scowl indicates differently. Shock pours into my body like lead, forcing my walk to grow more stolid with each step.

My representation of manliness sometimes feels like an ignominious detraction from the hegemonic conception of blackness. Thus I become chemically opposed to all of the people in my life. I have learned that racism does not depart in those moments wherein black people idly harm one another. As black masculinity is ipso facto racialized, the racism derives from how the cultural definition of blackness convinces me that I must abstain from authenticity in order to exist in my community at all. As a result, I fear some of the loving black people who constitute my world, and distance myself with that prejudice. Indeed, we remain unaware of how tragic and racist our intolerance is, as it becomes servile to this war that we entertain.

This realization informs how I interpret Panel 14, *Peace*. The cannon ostensibly and initially feels vestigial and antique. However, its basic purpose remains fearsomely the same, as a weapon of mass destruction.

Treating the vestigial cannon as metonymic for a declined preoccupation with warfare, Lawrence proffers that the American colonists may have deceived themselves into believing that foreign relations with Britain were peaceful and that thus these weapons were for the most part useless to them. But the deception does not successfully purify the weapon. Similarly, we as a modern black community have formed disadvantaged imaginations of racism. Our contestations were once a useful weapon of warfare, as during the Tuskegee Institute student movements to protest the murders of black people. This context is not condemnable; rather, it is honorable. However, we cannot forget the utility of reproach in warfare. Our community has reimagined that weapon as a vestige purely in situations that do not represent mainstream racism, such as in intracommunal affairs regarding those with intersectional identities. But our community is not so internally sound that the weapon withers; rather, the weapon of words proves to still be fearsome and destructive.

Looking at the painting, my pleasure at observing this withering weapon is gone. But there is still something to be gained. The piece activates in me a passion to dissolve barriers within my community because it illustrates the ultimate goal: the fantasy wherein disuse allows the menacing wartime instrument of words to sprout tantalizing flowers.

Kylie Vargas
(Schomburg Center for Research in Black Culture)

The American Dream

Response to Panel 5, *We have no property! We have no wives! No children! We have no city! No country! —petition of many slaves, 1773*

What am I?
A person or thing
Because you don't see me that way
I'm only useful if it gets you what you want
I'm only helpful when you say I'm helpful
I'm just another pawn in your chess game
WELL I AM NOT A PAWN!
You think I wanted this
To be in a society where
I'm discriminated against
You think I wanted to be your servant
You think I wanted to be illiterate
You think I wanted to be on that boat
You think I wanted to be black
Well I may never have wanted to be
These things, but why do you get to decide
All these things
About me
I'm not stupid
I'm not ignorant
I'm not lazy
I'm not loud
I'm not ugly
I'm not wretched
I'm me

But that's not good enough for you
You spout your words saying how
"We are equal"
Please explain that to me
Because ever since I came here
I never felt "equal"
Even the Constitution states
"All men are created equal"
But what about me?
Am I not the same as you?
I'm made of flesh and bones just like you!
Why am I perceived as less than?
And even after the 14th, 15th, and
16th amendments were passed
Nothing has changed
We are still discriminated against
And the cycle continues on for each
Future generation
Still fighting for the same thing
Why does history repeat itself?
Don't we all deserve something good
In our life?
All I wanted is a home, a job, and a family
Why is that so much to ask for?

CHAPTER THREE

STRUGGLE FOR POWER

Lynsey Borges (Boston Community Leadership Academy)

Chaos

Response to panel 24, *Of the Senate House, the President's Palace, the barracks, the dockyard…nothing could be seen except heaps of smoking ruins… —a British officer at Washington, 1814*

This painting reveals an intricate war scene with cannons being shot, but Jacob Lawrence chooses to focus on a dead bird. To me, the painting depicts the chaos of war and how anything can be affected by death. Seeing his representation of death, I feel a sense of compassion because I understand why he chose the bird as the symbol of a bigger picture. Panel 24 relates to the world now because far too often we see violence around us. We see people in our community fighting against each other in gangs, just like in the war Lawrence depicts. I often hear gun violence right outside my window, people shooting at each other. It makes me feel that as a society, we are failing each other. Yet at the same time, it helps me to stay focused on my goals even more.

Looking at the painting, I realize that seemingly insignificant things can represent a bigger picture. I also wonder about Lawrence's thought process and what his opinions would be on major issues from the past as they relate to problems in today's world. He drew a dead bird, and to me, the bird represents a deceased soldier, which reminds me of all those who have fought and died for their countries. In the end, death is a symbolic representation of chaos and the tragic outcome of war.

Tyler Burston (Schomburg Center for Research in Black Culture)

Revolutionary Confusion: Internal Conflicts and the Black Freedom Struggle

Response to Panel 5, *We have no property! We have no wives! No children! We have no city! No country! –petition of many slaves, 1773*

The power of this piece lies in its ability to illustrate some of the most complicated and divisive aspects of the black American experience in a singular image. The panel, cleaved in two by the clash of two factions opposed visually, physically, and ideologically, symbolizes the many conflicts that manifested themselves in black American narratives. As a stolen, oppressed, and dehumanized people, black Americans, simply by recognizing our own humanity, stand in conflict with those who wish to rob us of that humanity. Personally, it is easy for me to feel that I am in a perpetual state of war with white supremacy. Like other black Americans, I am perpetually vulnerable to the violence that white supremacy inspires, and thus combating it is an essential means of survival. This "war" is one that I have inherited, and with that inheritance comes a daunting body of questions regarding how this war is to be "fought." Which paths to freedom are the most effective? Which are the most ethical? Is structural reform or complete revolution the answer? Does virtue lie in violent revolt or nonviolent resistance?

The tragedy of the panel lies in the way it brings to mind these deeply challenging questions yet supplies no easy answers. In the image, we see a violent slave revolt, a physical manifestation of the war against white supremacy. The chaos, confusion, and suffering intrinsic to this form of war are evident in the strained faces and bloodied bodies of the revolting slaves, which contrast with the unscathed and faceless profiles of their enemies. The violence in the image is juxtaposed against its title. A quotation from the petition for freedom signed by a slave known as "Felix," the title represents the ideological opposite of the rebelling slaves. Felix decries violent revolution in favor of a direct appeal to a powerful man, nonviolently requesting that freedom be granted to him. The panel presents two conflicting ideologies, two ways of conducting "war" against white supremacy, and forces me to consider the consequences of both.

I can find little militaristic glory in the violence present in this art. The cruelly detailed images of black suffering in the painting are heartbreaking. They are a tragic reminder of the death and pain that pollute my people's story. I mourn every martyr of the war against white supremacy, from every ancestor murdered while rebelling to every child victimized by police brutality. There is a price to physical resistance, and I cannot welcome any war that will produce more black death. However, it's hard for me to celebrate the attitudes of those like Felix. How far can begging for our freedom truly take us? What use are these appeals if our oppressors ignore them? Do such appeals simply make our resistance palatable? Should freedom be asked for or taken?

Like the frame, split visually by the conflict of two factions, I often feel split internally by these questions, between multiple visions for a revolution. The revolution, however, is nonetheless necessary

Rashad Freeman (Schomburg Center for Research in Black Culture)

─────

The Theme of Struggle

─────

General response

The paintings in the *Struggle* series are symbolic, and each of them has a different meaning. What relates them all is the theme of struggle that certain groups of Americans faced on a daily basis, although they lived in a different time. We can see that oppression has been a theme over the course of American history. This exhibition interests me because this year in my AP United States history class we went over many of the topics that arose in Lawrence's work.

I recognized the Massachusetts Bay Colony, the Declaration of Independence, the Treaty of Paris, and immigration in the mid-1800s. One piece that especially caught my eye was the fifth panel, which depicts enslaved black men fighting for freedom. The painting shows the men in shackles using weapons to resist. Attached to the panel is a petition, made by a man identifying himself as "Felix," who challenged the governor of the Massachusetts Bay Colony for freedom. The painting reveals the violent and progressive approach to obtain freedom, while the petition proposed by Felix is an example of a nonviolent stance that can take longer to produce results. Civil rights activists including Reverend Martin Luther King, Jr., and Malcolm X constantly fought over whether to take a nonviolent or violent approach. There is a sense of both continuity and change in this painting.

From these panels, I learned about the struggles of the nation's people in early America and the impacts of those struggles. They opened my eyes to think more creatively and wonder why things are the way they are today. Panel 30 tells the story of a relatively unknown man and the struggles he endured. Morris Birkbeck, an English Quaker and abolitionist, traveled from the South to Illinois with the desire to improve the lives of the underprivileged. In the painting, an ox is seen hauling a wagon, which represents Birkbeck and his travels westward. Blood drips from the ox, suggesting the dedication, sacrifice, and weight of hardship Birkbeck endured. Lawrence's series is significant because it depicts human struggle, not pinpointing just one race or identity. It helps me appreciate not only the history of black people in America, but also the rich story of America itself, the sacrifices of all the people who immigrated to the New World and contributed to the creation of this country.

Zarina Lewin (Schomburg Center for Research in Black Culture)

Governing States

Response to Panel 15, *We, the people of the United States, in order to form a more perfect Union, establish justice, insure domestic tranquility…*
–17 September 1787

"Struggle" is a term used to emphasize the difficult hardships that challenge one's way of living. Struggle helps to develop the person who each of us becomes. However, it may also be the thing that brings us down. Jacob Lawrence's paintings portray visually the struggles that millions of people have had to endure. Struggle can change a person for better or for worse. As panel 15 of the *Struggle* series suggests, decisions can be a type of struggle, because making one mistake can affect multiple parties, with harmonious or devastating results. Trying to please everyone is another struggle.

If we focus on two aspects of the painting, we see how it involves struggle in government decisions. First, there are thirteen men who are working on the Constitution. They are sweating and look tired. Determining what to include in a constitution can be frustrating and time-consuming. These men struggle to decide what to do in order to maintain peace within all the states.

The second aspect to look at closely is in the front of the painting. The swords there represent how many men must vote in order to approve the Constitution. Seven out of the thirteen men must be on the same page. Not all people have the same opinion in a matter that involves not just them but others as well. A majority of the parties must agree, yet they all want to minimize any disadvantage to their own state. And while every man wants to gain benefits for his state, he does not want to anger the others.

This painting symbolizes the challenge and pain of working with others. All the participants give their own input and sometimes refuse to change their opinion, no matter what. Voting makes it even harder. In the end, debating with your peers can bring out the best in you. Adding your opinion to the debate can help you break out of your shell. I am an introvert and considering this helped me realize that having a voice is a good thing.

In the painting, only men are present. As a young woman, I think it would have been more fair to have both men and women in the room for this debate, to fully represent everyone, not just the men. Even today there are fewer roles for women. The world is made up of both genders.

Harry Osei-Bonsu (Studio Museum in Harlem)

The Struggle: Power

Response to Panel 17, *I shall hazard much and can possibly gain nothing by the issue of the interview… —Hamilton before his duel with Burr, 1804*

"Growth" is a loose term. People use the word to describe outcomes that are more favorable than those in the past, but who chooses what is favorable for a whole nation? Of course, those in power. Growth is like our fingerprints—unique to every person. What is growth for one person may be the fall of everything another stands for. The question of who should have power in society and who should not have it has been asked continually in history. This same question has led to war, violence, and ultimately growth, at least from my perspective. Jacob Lawrence's *Struggle* series resonates with my present because the paintings can be interpreted as a representation of universal human challenges. Although they are all great pieces of art, panel 17 struck me most.

On the left, Alexander Hamilton stands with his head bowed to the ground, clutching his fatal gunshot wound, while Aaron Burr stands hidden in the shadows; a plant protrudes from a crack in the ground. With this painting Lawrence opened a conversation about the struggle for power in American history. From the civil rights movement to the Stonewall riots, power has always been one of the main topics in our country's discourse. Burr and Hamilton's duel demonstrates just how important power is: Burr was willing to kill his rival and ultimately end his own political career because he opposed him. Hamilton even went so far as to risk his life so that Burr wouldn't get into office, although even he, in his final will, acknowledged how senseless that was.

This was not the last time America would see such a battle. Other figures, such as Martin Luther King, Jr., and Marsha P. Johnson, would walk directly into danger to assert their power. Lawrence captured the continuity and nuance of this ongoing clash by depicting one of the most famous and early struggles for power in America. The only outlier in this painting, however, is the plant that grows out of the earth. Why would Lawrence add a symbol of life and growth in a painting that is mainly about death and struggle? In a painting, every single aspect and brushstroke is intentional, from size to color choice. The scene of Hamilton and Burr seems juxtaposed to the plants and trees in the background and foreground. This can be seen in the differing color choice; the men are very dark and intense, while the plants are lighter and calmer. It's almost as if they were meant to attract more attention than Hamilton and Burr. Perhaps they were?

The struggle for power in America comes about through individual activism and protest, which influence movements and lead to change. Jacob Lawrence provides a means to look at America's history critically, without considering race, ethnicity, or gender. The transfer of power in America has often occurred through violence and bloodshed; Lawrence's choice of a duel to comment about this clash is both nuanced and necessary.

Yoilett Ramos Sanchez (Boston Community Leadership Academy)

The "Tragic" Incident of 1812

Response to panel 19, *Thousands of American citizens have been torn from their country and from everything dear to them: they have been dragged on board ships of war of a foreign nation. –Madison, 1 June 1812*

Panel 19 of Jacob Lawrence's *Struggle* series shows four American men being held captive by British soldiers. The sailors are tied up tightly with thick black rope and are bleeding from wounds. The rich, red liquid that circulates in our arteries is running down their pants and skin onto the floor of the boat. This must have been a traumatic moment for these men, standing in front of the British leader, whose posture reveals a sense of certainty: certain he is in control, certain what his next plan is going to be. He holds a sword which establishes his authority. In the background, you can see the backstay of the boat and the big sail. The leader looks at the sailors with disgust; the three thick black lines on his face near his eye, cheek, and nose indicate his age. His mouth is formed downward along with his eyes, which are nearly covered by his blue lid. I imagine the British leaders on the boat discussing how they will use the American sailors for their

own benefit. This makes me think of the issue of the United States selling firearms to Saudi Arabia, leading them to target innocent civilians in Yemen. Forces in Yemen use child soldiers, and these children have no freedom of choice, just like the men in the picture.

It would be a lie to say I feel nothing toward this work. As a person of color, I feel like someone who has gotten revenge but feels bad about it later. In this painting, I am essentially looking at white people experiencing what they have been doing to my ancestors for centuries. I think about how in this case, it was done by their own race. How they felt to be captive. The men's arms are bound so tightly by the rope that you can see they are turning blue.

But revenge is not what I actually feel because these men were held captive and made to feel inferior by their own race. Today, unfortunately, minorities often make each other feel inferior instead of uplifted; and we can't make white people feel lesser, only they can. If white people experienced oppression among their own race, I am guessing they would feel this way. This thought creates an unfulfilled pit in my stomach. Marginalized people in the United States are giving white people what they want, which is to turn on ourselves. The question that comes up for me is, if white people turned on each other like people of color do, would everyone be equal?

Lucia Santos (Seattle Art Museum)

A Quiet Struggle in the Static

Response to Panel 13, *Victory and Defeat*

When I first viewed Jacob Lawrence's *Victory and Defeat* (1955), it did not strike a chord with me. I noticed how some of the colors were strangely calm next to the harsh black of the cannonballs. It only made me feel uneasy, nothing more. I continued to the next paintings in the series, depicting the excruciating intersections of history and change, where women fired guns and people staggered on battlefields—the energy far more frenetic.

Yet I found myself returning to *Victory and Defeat*. Alongside the dynamic environments of the other panels in the series, this image continued to strike me as a stagnant one. When I really took the time to see it on its own, however, I found a quiet struggle in the static.

In the baby-blue egg-tempera air between those two gray hands is power. Power is blue, and cold, and sharp. Power is a sword, in Lawrence's vision. Power given from one party to a new one, held and passed on. Between those hands there is apprehension, similar to what one witnesses in the other panels. But different in that no drastic movements are made to demonstrate it; simply the gravity of the two hands, together and apart.

Within this painting's stillness, I interpret turmoil, but I sense complacency, too. The two hands are each giving and receiving power, in a never-ending cycle. When struggle is less visible, complacency thrives. It is the space between victory and defeat, when one is stuck in a system or cycle, never seeing or seeking broader, deeper liberation. In my own life, I find myself slipping into apathy when I feel removed from the pain of others. In my country, I feel it increasing as I read horrifying stories of people in deep pain at the border. Through a screen, I share parts of my identity with some of the people whose painful stories are broadcast out into a digital void; reaching out for empathy, justice, anger, anything but my complicit silence. Still, I keep scrolling.

Victory and Defeat feels clear yet ambiguous. Power is shared but remains in gray hands. Power remains a weapon. Soft colors contrast a pile of cannonballs ready to inflict pain on the next group that might rise up and threaten the present hierarchy. The hand receiving once threatened the rule of the hand that gives. True liberation is hard to find, and just as tedious to seek.

I see power turn into complacency when old societal systems remain intact. Revisions of these systems, ever so slight and oppression pristinely kept in place. I see apathy seeping into my mind and the minds of those around me as we are further removed from the struggles of others. We move forward, convincing ourselves that we are progressing, when in reality we are leaving power in the same places. And as in stagnant water, we settle into decay.

CHAPTER FOUR

STRUGGLE FOR A VOICE

Mya Barnhart (Phillips Collection/Thurgood Marshall Academy)

Suffering in Silence

Response to Panel 27, *…for freedom we want and will have, for we have served this cruel land long enuff…*
—a Georgia slave, 1810

"Suffering in silence"
A way to describe a tortured mind.
A silenced soul bound to a promise passed
Down from generation to generation.
A promise to keep your white feelings
Inside of you,
To let them torture you,
Until you die.

Your white feelings
Are abnormal,

Not black enough
Or not at all.
We don't believe in depression,
Anxiety,
Schizophrenia,
PTSD,
OCD.
Foreign objects that are not accepted
In our community.
Weapons against our strength
And perseverance as a race.
We've made it through slavery
And racial segregation.
Why can't we make it through
A few sad feelings,
Or constant stress,
Or the constant need for order?
I commend our ancestors for those
Beautiful struggles
For freedom (or at least the idea of it).
Yet we are not free from this stigma.
It's like two men
Pinning us down.
We're trying to fight back,
Gain control
But such is a loss.
Our mind is the
Tortured black soul in between those men.
The stigma is the rifle stabbing our minds,
Injuring us,
Weakening us.
Picture this to be a revolt,
A failed one.
A false uprising.

Unfortunately, we can't use depression
As an excuse

As to why we killed a classroom full of people.
But they can.
We can't say our anxiety is the reason why we
Walked in a church and opened fire
Fueled by rage,
Racism,
And the intent to kill.
But they can.
We can't use schizophrenia as the reason why
We would shoot up a Walmart full of
Unsuspecting shoppers
With mission to purge as many Hispanics
Out of this country because
We as the shooter feel they should not be here.
But they can.
Their "Declaration of Independence" says
That Britain's tyrannical rule should
Be abolished
"For transporting us beyond…to be tried for
Pretended offenses."
Yet they are quick to detain or kill us for
The smallest crimes.
We cannot sell cigarettes,
Sell CDs,
Be at a public park,
Or even be on our own property
Without being harassed or arrested.
If we are detained we are being transported
To either a morgue
Or a kangaroo court.
Do not forget
The "Declaration of Independence"
Was written for independence for
All that was white.
Our ancestors were not included in
That declaration.

Zora Danticat (Schomburg Center for Research in Black Culture)

Wind and Debris Soar Past

Response to Panel 5, *We have no property! We have no wives! No children! We have no city! No country! —petition of many slaves, 1773*

Wind and debris soar past
Telling me to go back
I am enveloped in the beauty of this storm
That I cannot obtain.
Weep not, for you will be silenced
The storm rages on despite my plea
To cease its tears
Those tears, so clear and beautiful
I breathe in icy particles and dust that

Attack my lungs
I sink deeper into unconsciousness and yet
The beauty of the colors of the storm
Silences me instead
I dance with the wind that pushes me back
I cry with the tearful clouds
I sing with the debris that cracks and distorts my body
My despair will become the fingernails
That claw at the throat
Of the sadness of
My brothers and me
Until I am no longer "human"
But I am one with the storm that lasts for ages.

Emily Deosaran (Metropolitan Museum of Art)

You Have the Belief

Response to Panel 28, *Immigrants admitted from all countries: 1820 to 1840–115,773*

You live half your childhood as average but you don't realize it. You feel special because you're a child; you have the belief that you're going to do something great in life. You'll make something of yourself no matter what, somehow. Then you move to the Big Apple, the place of opportunity, and you think to yourself, It's finally happening—the first step to making something of yourself. You start a new school with a bunch of kids who look just like you; your mom thought it would make adjusting easier. You try to make friends and realize they're nothing like you. They were born here. You're an immigrant. You grew up differently. Different accent. Different attitude. Different school routine. Yet they look just like you.

You brush it off, go to class and pay attention as you would back home. You think they're going slow because you're new to the class and they want you to catch up. You raise your hand and tell the teacher she doesn't need to. She looks as if she's contemplating whether you are serious or simply being pretentious. After settling with the latter, she tells you to sit down quietly and pay attention. Confused but polite, you agree. Then you think about back home, where you learned these things in first grade, or standard 1 to you, you think back to how differently the teachers taught, you think about your friends, you think about how confusing everything is. You go home and tell your mom. The next day she comes to school and talks to your principal about a placement test. The principal replies that it's not available and moving you to a higher grade will just make you lonely. But you already feel lonely.

You easily take advantage of the situation by not having to try at all for the next two years. All of a sudden it's time to start middle school, but you're so accustomed to not trying that you begin to slack off. Surprisingly, when you slack off it doesn't affect your grades that much. You remain respectful to teachers, so they always have good things to report home. Soon enough your mom doesn't bother checking up on your school anymore because you're "doing fine." Then things become harder and you need to catch yourself, so you begin to try really hard again. But it's a bit too late, because there's lots of competition. You're doing great but it's not enough; you're accustomed to doing better than others without even trying, and you begin to lose the motivation.

Before you know, it's high school and things get even harder. You know you definitely can't slack off, and you can't let your mom know, since she trusted you.

Now you're stuck in an internal struggle and you wonder what things would have been like if you had just stayed home.

Jennifer Hernandez (Metropolitan Museum of Art)

Silent Cry

Response to Panel 11, *120.9.14.286. 9.33 -ton 290.9.27 be at 153.9.28.110. 8.19.255.9.29 evening 178.9.8…*
—an informer's coded message

Bundles of whispers are buried from the
Youth. No matter the burden that comes
With the truth. The wrinkled stay silent till
Their tomb.
The children scream.
Hear our cry.
As the youth grow,
Watered by deceit,
No guilt is felt,
No tides are lowered.
Only overflowed by the youths' desire
Of knowledge.

The elders only see naive toddlers,
And feed them secrets.
Teach us the history of our African roots,
To love our history,
To nurture our coils created by you.
Teach us to love ourselves.

You told us stories that were meant to
"Protect" and "heal,"
To fabricate worlds of silence,
Happiness,
But fibs do not last,
Hear our cry
Though it sounds like a whisper in the
World of adults,
Love is love.
Stop being blinded by color.
"Norms" of gender only simulate unacceptance.
The youth are falling
Our hurt ain't fading,
In all the white noise we plead,
Hear Our Cry!

Ahmed Iginla (Metropolitan Museum of Art)

The Devil to the Ears

General response

A single story is the devil to the ears. Have you ever wanted to tell your story, but for the good of others, you never shared it? The other side will never be heard, and if there is an uproar, it becomes a murmur—then utter silence.

False Narrative
Now you are inadvertently sharing that message to all who hear. Not knowing the poison you have embedded in their minds. I mean, it's all you know.

Pressure

As it rises you're pushed to speak, but it quickly dies down as the opposers force a narrative down your throat. You're forced to glue your lips in fear of consequences, I mean, it's all you know.

Societal Norms

Are these really societal norms, or just a way to cover up your insecurities? Where I'm from, it's either you play ball or you're in the streets. What if you take another route? That's rare when you're only getting one story, one narrative of how things should be. A lot of people fall into this trap, I mean, it's all you know.

Story

Imagine a young boy who grew up only around girls. Raised by a single mother with four kids, all girls except for me. My eyes would always absorb my sisters' actions, and it would make the wheels of my mind turn. I probably couldn't join them because of my mother. She didn't approve, fearing I would become feminine just by doing what my sisters were doing. Sometimes I would wonder what the issue was to grow my hair out and get braids, I mean it was the style back then, the other boys were getting these haircuts. She couldn't blame me, I mean, it's all I knew.

What's Next?

In today's society there are a lot of false narratives that pressure people to follow societal norms. It is okay to be different, and you find your own path to create your own story, no one else's. Now think, is it really all YOU know?

Makayla Jordan (Birmingham Museum of Art)

Slave To

General response

Haven't wrote a poem in a while.
It's because a few
Nights ago…I cried so
Hard
My throat sung those old
Slave songs cause lately
I guess I've been a slave to perfection,
A slave to the image, unable
To smile if not requested, unable to escape.
Tried to listen to those revolutionaries on Twitter
Like Frederick Douglass and such.
Only made me fear the freedom
That might not ever be.

Kioni Shropshire-Maina (Studio Museum in Harlem)

What I Am Afraid to Lose

General response

The whole time I am leaving this place
Called home,
I feel the heavy press of my brother's hands
On my shoulders fading and fading
Until I am alone
Desperately grasping at all
That has been taken from me
And I am afraid of losing what
I have already lost:
My language, my customs, my girlhood
Sold into worn, pale hands
What I am afraid of losing I stir into
The red paint of my people
And spread high across my cheekbones
I am hoping my mother's spirits will see
This and know me
What I am afraid of losing I whisper between
The roots of foreign trees
And into the eddies of rivers that wander

Back towards home
I press each familiar thing into my son's hands
So he too will know the feel of it
I hold each precious word on my tongue
So I do not forget the taste of it
I hold each precious word in my heart until
I can come home once more
And I do find home again
Years of wandering with white men pass
And it is the breaking
And un-breaking of my heart all at once
Stood nose to nose with all that
I have left behind,
I spread my collection of words out
In front of my brother like an offering and
I have nothing left to lose anymore
My brother's hands pressing into
My shoulders once again
My mother's spirits hearing me once more

CHAPTER FIVE

STRUGGLE TO SURVIVE

Sophie Fishman (Metropolitan Museum of Art)

I Examined the Room Around Me

General response

I examined the room around me: each face glistened in the stifling New York summer heat, eyes downcast. We sat silently and watched the minutes tick by. A loud and definite knock on the door came to my attention. My father slowly pressed his hands into our worn crimson sofa, pushed himself to a standing position, and went to open the door. He returned with a visitor, my rabbi. She turned to us, sympathetically, and told us how much of an honor it was to be presiding over a funeral for a survivor.

When I got the phone call from my mother saying that my grandmother had passed away at Mount Sinai Hospital that morning, I thought of her house, in Flushing,

Queens. It was yellowed, modestly furnished, and somehow always smelled like Hebrew National kosher hot dogs. The wallpaper was peeling, the piano was out of tune, and dust would appear on your fingers if you even thought of playing it. But her house was where I felt safe. Scattered around were photographs of my dad and uncle when they had goatees and full heads of hair, on the fridge were my school pictures dating back to kindergarten, and in the basement was my mother's wedding dress, waiting for my turn.

But now, here was this word, "survivor." When I brought it up, she would turn away, not wanting to pass on the trauma of her childhood to her grandchildren. So I relied on my father. He told me stories of my grandmother masquerading as a Christian, hanging crosses on her wall and praising a God she didn't believe in, in order to survive in a place where her very existence was a crime. Stories of family members being taken away to camps, never to be heard from again. He told of her entire village being decimated, people shot like dogs, bleeding, lifeless, and left rotting on the ground.

He also told me about my grandmother's coming to America. She spoke only broken English and came with only her mother and sister. They moved into a Bronx apartment under the tracks of the 4 train. She was tasked with creating a new sense of normalcy in a country and a city that were unfamiliar to her. Though she was nearly seventeen years old, she enrolled herself in first grade. The shame she felt for being the oldest in her class was greatly outweighed by her desire to learn and her drive to create a new life for herself, away from the struggle of her youth.

When I first heard my grandmother's story, I had a difficult time reconciling the two truths I held about her: the loving, warm figure I'd always known and loved, and the resilient survivor I became acquainted with after her death. But one string that tied her story together was her fiery desire to live. It was her drive that enabled her to survive one of the greatest horrors the world has seen. And it was her drive to live life fully that inspired her to start a family and pass down her faith and insist that it never failed her, despite what it had cost her.

Alyse Gaskins
(Phillips Collection/Thurgood Marshall Academy)

Damaged Souls and Broken Bones

Response to Panel 25, *I cannot speak sufficiently in praise of the firmness and deliberation with which my whole line received their approach…*
—Andrew Jackson, New Orleans, 1815

The Battle of New Orleans, the last conflict of the War of 1812, took place on January 8, 1815. The Americans were outnumbered by the British, but still were victorious, leaving the enemy troops running with blood, lined up against their fallen ladder. The war had officially ended on December 24, 1814, when the United States and the United Kingdom signed the Treaty of Ghent, but unfortunately the news had not yet reached America

The war was vicious; both sides fought hard for victory and praise. War is what makes the world so bad. I feel that war is not really needed to prove a point. War creates a lot of unnecessary economic problems. It can lead to displacement of citizens and post-traumatic stress disorder and other mental illnesses. Panel 25 evokes many emotions for me; it makes me feel many things. Damaged souls and broken bones hurt both physically and mentally. Bloodstains, slaughtered beings. The deadly aftermath hits deep for just about everyone.

Aggression is never a good way to solve conflict, and it does nothing but create more conflict. Looking at this painting, I think of only sadness, pain, and hurt. Simple conversation, communication, or negotiation, instead of violence, could help resolve differences.

The painting shows the complex aftermath of the war and how deadly it was, and how the world was back then and how it still is. In the United States, we have always dealt with war against other countries, and it's crazy how this problem is still present. Victory isn't really victory if you're taking lives. War is completely uncalled for, and this painting defines the true hurt and turmoil it can cause among people.

Amya Hudson (Phillips Collection/Thurgood Marshall Academy)

A Feeling of Perseverance

Response to Panel 27,...*for freedom we want and will have, for we have served this cruel land long enuff...* *—a Georgia slave, 1810*

Two white males fighting two black males. The struggle in Jacob Lawrence's painting depicts the ongoing racism and violence that black people have had to endure for centuries. The work shows the strength that black people have had to maintain in order to overcome their hardships. When I look at this painting, it reminds me of their perseverance. "For freedom we want and will have, for we have served this cruel land long enuff..." These words from a Georgia slave show the yearning for liberty. Black people had to disregard their own wants and needs for those of their oppressors every day. Knowing this makes me see them as strong individuals, fighting to make it through each day.

When I look at this painting, I also think of an epigraph from the book *Chains* by Laurie Halse Anderson: "I also have been whipped many a time on my naked skin, and sometimes till the blood has run down over my waistband; but the greatest grief I then had was to see them whip my mother, and to hear her, on her knees, begging for mercy." These words by the Reverend David George reflect on his horrific childhood as a slave. Nobody should have had to go through anything like that. The Declaration of Independence states, "We hold these truths to be self-evident, that all men are created equal," but these "men" did not include black people. In today's society, white-on black crime is still an important and relevant topic. African Americans are cautious to step out into predominantly white areas for fear of being harassed or having physical encounters. Police brutality is a serious issue everywhere in the United States. The police often target black people and make a small situation into something bigger. Two hundred forty-three years after the signing of the Declaration of Independence, African Americans are not treated as equals.

Under slavery, some slaves fought back. They wanted change. This painting depicts a failed rebellion to liberate enslaved people. It prompts me to think of one of the most successful slave revolts, led by Nat Turner. In August 1831, Southampton County, Virginia, was a place of chaos. Nat Turner believed that if he wanted freedom, he would have to take it himself. He and his followers killed at least fifty-one people during their rebellion. As I write, according to *The New York Times*, 623 people have been killed by the police in the United States thus far in 2019 alone. A large portion of these were African American. In today's society, people show their concern and frustration for this treatment by protesting. Most demonstrations start peacefully, but they often get ugly when justice is not served—as in the case of the death of Freddie Gray. Gray, an African American, died after being arrested by Baltimore police officers in April 2014. After his death, people marched and some protests turned very violent. Nonetheless, we will continue to fight for our rights and march for black lives until we gain equality and put an end to hate and racism.

Makenda Marc (Boston Community Leadership Academy)

Separation

Response to Panel 18, *In all your intercourse with the natives, treat them in the most friendly and conciliatory manner which their own conduct will admit… —Jefferson to Lewis & Clark, 1803*

every time he visited, a sense of joy filled my heart. We caught up on so much and he gave many hugs and greetings to other family members. It was a celebration every time he visited, and each time he left, I felt empty and lonely. In a world where family members are getting separated from each other—whether by our immigration system or foster care system—getting to see our loved ones every day is precious. For those who cannot, it causes grief and sadness.

In panel 18 of Jacob Lawrence's *Struggle* series, Native people are assembled together wearing bright-colored clothing, representing a moment of joy and reunion. This painting describes the emotions and relief experienced when two loved ones, Sacajawea and her brother, Cameahwait, reunite with one another after a long absence.

I connect to this feeling of reuniting with family. When I lived in Haiti as a five-year-old, my father, who lived in America, came to visit my brother and me once a year, and

Munaja Mehzabin (Metropolitan Museum of Art)

Freedom Muslims Want and Will Have

Response to Panel 27,...*for freedom we want and will have, for we have served this cruel land long enuff...*
–a Georgia slave, 1810

It was nine in the morning on September 11, 2001, and I was getting ready to leave the house. All the phones were ringing. Everyone was telling us to turn on the news. We all dropped everything we were doing. We couldn't believe our own eyes. None of us had ever seen anything like this before. We were scared and we didn't know what to do. Later that day, my parents and I talked.

"Amira, do you know who attacked the Twin Towers?" my dad asked.

"Yeah, terrorists," I said, confused.

"Yes, but they were Muslims, and we're Muslim," my mom said.

"Okay, guys, get to the point," I said.

I heard my mom sigh.

"Just be careful at school tomorrow, we live in a cruel world, you never know what could happen," my dad said.

"I'll be perfectly fine. I've got my friends. They all have my back. Don't worry." At least that's what I thought.

"If anything happens, call us right away!" my mom said.

"All right, good night!" I headed to my room. They were worried for nothing, no one ever had a reason to hate me.

September 12 was an odd day. In the morning, I got ready like it was any other day. I typically walked to school with my friend Samantha, but she didn't call.

I was used to seeing my friends, but I didn't see them all day. It felt like everyone was avoiding me. Then I remembered what my parents had said, and everything clicked.

I remember being relieved hearing the last bell ring. I just wanted to go home. I was heading out of the building when I heard someone shout. "Hey, towelhead!" What the hell is a towelhead?

"I'm talking to you, terrorist!" I turned to see who was shouting, and there were my best friends and my friend Lindsay's boyfriend, Todd.

"Where have you guys been all day?" I asked.

"Why is she talking to us?" Lindsay said. I was in shock—my parents were right. I never thought I'd see the day when my friends would turn their backs on me.

I started walking away. I just wanted to get home at this point.

"Don't walk away from us!" Todd shouted. I felt someone pull my hijab off.

"What's wrong with you? I never even did anything to you! Leave me alone!" I screamed.

"Oh, yeah? Your people killed my dad!" Todd said. The next thing I knew, I was pushed onto the floor.

"Stop!" I shouted. They all started hitting me. They wouldn't stop. I couldn't move. I lay there for so long until someone came and helped me.

I was lying in bed, thinking I had done something wrong. I let people get into my head; I felt like the bad guy. Then I realized that none of this was my fault. Even if someone were to blame me a million times, it wouldn't change the fact that I was innocent. I knew then that things would happen in life, and I would face struggles. It's how I deal with them that matters.

Abena Manuh (Schomburg Center for Research in Black Culture)

Self-Struggle and Perceptions

Response to Panel 15, *We, the people of the United States, in order to form a more perfect Union, establish justice, insure domestic tranquility…* *–17 September 1787*

Indeed I will overcome
Although five fingers are never the same
They support each other
I'll fight this battle with my strength and might
For hardship and pain I have to endure
I shouldn't be defined by other people's
Perspective of my struggle
Wondering how pain and sweat
Made a difference
Leading to a firm and independent me
I'll let the world know

That my fearless and courageous me has
Made me who I am
Working day and night to achieve
Making it possible to tell a painful story
Let the crowd talk ill or good
My sweat has made me laugh, cry, and smile

I wrote this poem to reflect on how humans
Struggle in life but never want to give up
Because society has made us believe that
Success is obtained from sweat and not
Just acquired.

Lindsey Ruiz (Schomburg Center for Research in Black Culture)

Toxicity in Today's Society

Response to Panel 15, *We, the people of the United States, in order to form a more perfect Union, establish justice, insure domestic tranquility…* *–17 September 1787*

The way I understand this painting in our time is through the divisions among the people around me. The amount of stigma surrounding certain things, like politics, people's backgrounds and behaviors, and what we see in the media creates a lot of tension. In the painting, the visual tension between the black drapery and contrasted yellow-gold color within the people makes me think of the toxicity in today's society.

The human brain takes a tenth of a second to form what we call a "first impression," by looking at someone's face, for instance. Judgment is the instinct that helps us feel safe but can also be the cause for separation. All people have their own story, all of us are guarded by walls that we put up for protection. These walls are one of the first things we see. When we walk around with these masks to protect ourselves, we avoid truly connecting with others. We work hard for what we want to achieve, but we struggle with navigating the people we see every day.

In this panel, the sweat of the characters reminds me of what brings me peace. We are looking at thirteen men sweating and gesturing dramatically as they

debate how the people should be governed. Not only can this be directly related to today's political controversies, but it can be related to conflicts within ourselves. Tending to our own conflicts and disregarding the problems of those around us allow us to target one another for our own security.

As a young Hispanic teenager, I've witnessed tensions among my friends, family, and peers. It's easy to get caught up in myself, but I try to stop and observe the world around me. I sort through perspectives that compete with my own. They question the roles of people I look up to as examples and help me learn more about myself. Current events challenge me as a young woman, calling me to speak out about topics that force me to stand my ground, such as the gender wage gap, abortion laws, and hate crimes. The title …*in order to form more perfect Union* reads to me like something the artist wanted. I feel I connected to this painting because, reflecting on the society I live in, I also want unity and peace.

Lola Simon
(Metropolitan Museum of Art)

Rules of a Duel; or Growing Up

Response to Panel 17, *I shall hazard much and can possibly gain nothing by the issue of the interview…*
—Alexander Hamilton before his duel with Aaron Burr, 1804

Late summer. The sun is long gone but the remnants of heat make our clothes stick to our skin like taffy. We lie in the grass of your backyard; the stars lie suspended above us. They remind me of the plastic stars we put on the ceiling of your room years ago—the ones you found in the back of some store and slipped into your backpack when no one was looking. One day we danced in your room and they all came crashing down. I wonder whether, if we danced now, these stars would also fall.

We're silent—everything's silent, actually, except for the faint sound of crickets playing a song for no one. I turn to you.

"Promise you'll take care of yourself when I'm gone," I whisper to you.

You roll over to face me.

"If you promise you'll take care of yourself."

"I'm serious. Promise me."

"All right, I promise. I'll protect myself. I'll protect you. I'll protect the crickets, for god's sake. You don't have to worry about me."

You'd been growing more and more distant lately. I couldn't tell if I believed you anymore.

"Can you keep things light for once?" you grumble. "Summer's practically over. Let's just have fun."

I sigh.

"When I was younger I used to think that the craters on the moon were filled with mice," you tell me. You've always been so good at changing the subject. I don't feel like pushing it this time.

"How would mice even survive on the moon?" I respond finally.

"They're special moon mice."

I make out the faint features of your face in the darkness. You're smiling, your eyes scrunched up in the corners.

"You know, if we shout loud enough maybe they'll hear us," I tell you.

"I bet they will."

"What should we shout?"

"How about just 'hello?' " you suggest.

"Perfect."

We stand up onto our tiptoes, our chins pointed upwards. The word fills up the air, sinks into the ground. We both know there's no one left to listen.

Last night I dream I saw you again. It's been years since that last summer. I turn away from you and walk forward ten paces. I hold a gun; the metal of it burns my palm. Three counts. I spin around and raise the gun to shoot. It fires. Time hangs like the branches of a willow tree. As I face you I realize I stand before a child, your knuckles wrapped around the plastic handle of a water gun, finger on the useless trigger.

I wake. My bedsheets are soaked with sweat. The moon has stretched itself across my bedroom floor. I walk to the window and pull back the curtains. In the night there is stillness, the only sound the faint hum of crickets. This time I am sure they are playing for us. I listen, in my bedroom, where the paint peels off the walls. Perhaps you do too, wherever else exists beyond here.

Yael Torres
(Seattle Art Museum)

The False Hope of the "American Dream"

Response to Panel 28, *Immigrants admitted from all countries: 1820 to 1840—115,773*

When I think of all of the immigrants from various countries, I picture my mother's hometown, Pareo, Mexico. Like many parents, my mother left our native land and traveled three thousand miles to ensure that her children would have opportunities she previously could only dream of. When a *coyote* (one of the contacts in a network that stretches from Central America to Texas) let her know about the land of the free, she took her kids and followed him to the States.

When I think of all those who were deceived by the false hope of the "American Dream," I imagine immigrant parents suffering from silenced loneliness, neglect, and denial. Many of them went from a world filled with friends and a strong support base to unfamiliar territory, surrounded by uninterested neighbors and nameless coworkers met through labor facilities that pay under the table. Nevertheless, my mother doesn't dwell on the past. She smiles and shakes her head when you ask about her life back in our pueblo.

When I think of immigrant children, I think about how my silence bleeds a different shade of retaliation from that of my siblings and undocumented friends. As a first-generation American, I feel that my internal struggles revolve around dismantling patriarchal and oppressive systems, the recognition of my privilege as a documented dual citizen, and transgenerational trauma passed through the Indigenous soil and roots.

When I think of all the immigrants who want their freedom back, I think of the voices buried underneath the weight of the colonialism from which America benefited. The country asserts itself as an economic powerhouse while refusing to be held accountable for its injustices. Viewing this supposed melting pot's history through rose-colored glasses does not erase the suffering and forced labor of enslaved African Americans, nor the massive genocide of Indigenous American tribes, nor the continued erasure of LGBTQIA+ communities. These repeated practices echo throughout the history of this capitalist country, seemingly intent on distorting the efforts of the oppressed. What remains are those full after being fed prejudice from the spoon of white supremacy.

When I think about the rhetoric of fear surrounding immigrants, I think about how imagination causes fear, and how imagination is the source of all emotions. We imagine because we don't know what to expect. So when I imagine all of the immigrants admitted from all countries, I smile at the thought that maybe the barbarism and transgressions against us have equal and opposite reactions to something better happening in this world, some great swell of openness and wakefulness out there.

Johnná Nicole-Lynn Townes (Metropolitan Museum of Art)

Dirt

Response to Panel 26,
Peace

I had seen these flowers before. They looked familiar in a way that most flowers do, though I was never quite fond of flowers. When I was younger, my sister gave a bouquet to my mother, and I asked her if I could smell them. She held them out to me with a look of approval and I got excited because I had never smelled flowers before. On TV, people always smiled and breathed in deeply when they got flowers. I dipped my head into the bouquet and inhaled deeply through my nose. Almost immediately, without much thought, I said, "Ew, those smell like dirt!" My mom smacked my arm and it stung a little; she looked around to see if my sister had heard—she had not—and said, "No, they don't. Be quiet, they are a gift from your sister."

Thinking back on it now, I see that that event, those flowers, were a precursor for my life. If you look at flowers, you don't see struggle; in fact, I see the opposite: they just grow unapologetically, and for whatever reason, we dub them beautiful. A flower by any other name to me would still smell just as dirty; but I know now to keep that to myself. Other things aren't so clear. As I get older, things get more complicated. I speak after thinking for a long time and still say the wrong thing. No matter how cautious I am, I always step right on someone's toes. No one smacks me and tells me that I've done something wrong; they just talk behind my back or wrinkle their noses, and I'm left wondering what I've done. Scrambling to pick up the pieces, although they poke fun at me for doing so. Each piece like a flower petal in the hands of an impressionable girl. Do they like me? Do they like me not? Do they like me? Do they like me not? Although I've calculated the answer over and over again in my head, the pieces just don't add up. I swear it's like they have all gotten manuals on how to function, and I show up unprepared, wishing someone would just smack me, not knowing they already have. When they laugh at me it stings.

I find strange comfort in flowers, though, not because they are pretty or because they smell "nice," but because there is struggle in the soil. People walk all over it, they disregard it, and some years, there are no flowers. Yet some years, in the right season, there are. The ground receives all the right signals and gives them all back correctly, and flowers bloom. Maybe that's why they smell like dirt.

Kori Valentine (Phillips Collection/Thurgood Marshall Academy)

Doing What They Have to Do

Response to Panel 7, *The summer soldier and the sunshine patriot will, in this crisis, shrink from the service of his country. –Thomas Paine, 1776*

"The fear lived on in their practiced bop, their slouching denim, their big T-shirts, the calculated angle on their baseball caps, a catalog of behaviors and garments enlisted to inspire the belief that these boys were in firm possession of everything they desired," Ta-Nehisi Coates wrote in *Between the World and Me*. When I read this passage, I think about panel 7 from Jacob Lawrence's *Struggle* series. The title of the painting quotes from *The American Crisis*, Thomas Paine's series of revolutionary pamphlets. The painting shows men standing in snow, wearing coats and blankets and holding weapons. The characters remind me of kids standing on the corners doing what they have to do to survive in today's society. Just in Washington, DC, there were 160 reported deaths by homicide in 2018. Through mid-December of that year, 534 people were shot in the District, according to the *Washington Post*. Many of them were shot because of gang violence. Like in revolutionary times, gangs are created because people join together to fight back and protect their own. Another way this painting relates to the modern day is through gun violence.

The Declaration of Independence states that the British king "has constrained our fellow citizens taken captive on the high seas to bear arms against their country, to become the executioners of their friends and brethren, or to fall themselves by their hands." When people today fall into gangs or are "taken captive," they're given weapons to kill their brothers, sisters, and friends. It's all a trap: they can do as they're told and that leads to their downfall, or they don't do as told and it still leads to their downfall. This highlights the vulnerability of black teenagers.

"The summer soldier and the sunshine patriot will, in this crisis, shrink from the service of their country," Thomas Paine wrote in late 1776. Lawrence used this quotation because it represented the fact that Americans were trying to escape the tyranny of the British. He noticed the irony in Paine's urgent call for freedom and decided that his painting would also symbolize an urgency for freedom.

STRUGGLE: FROM THE HISTORY OF THE AMERICAN PEOPLE

JACOB LAWRENCE'S PAINTINGS

Austen Barron Bailly, Lydia Gordon, and Elizabeth Hutton Turner

Over the course of his career, Jacob Lawrence painted ten historical narratives. All of them are intact in public collections except one—his seventh series, the thirty-panel *Struggle: From the History of the American People* (1954–56), last seen in its totality in 1958. The dispersal of the paintings over time not only broke apart the series, but also lessened its narrative value because the images were separated from their original title captions, the words Lawrence chose to accompany each painting.

Thanks to the exhibition at the Peabody Essex Museum, twenty-five of the *Struggle* paintings have been accounted for, while five remain unlocated. We present the known works alongside reproductions of the missing paintings, along with all the original title captions. For two paintings, there is no known image. Each work is painted in egg tempera on hardboard and measures 12 × 16 or 16 × 12 inches.

Panel 1

...is life so dear or peace so sweet as to be purchased at the price of chains and slavery? —Patrick Henry, 1775

The *Struggle* series began with this painting when it was first exhibited in December 1956. For its title caption, Lawrence selected the closing line of a speech given by attorney and orator Patrick Henry to the second Virginia Convention in Richmond, Virginia, on March 23, 1775. Henry's defense of American colonists' freedom galvanized the patriots to demand liberty from the British. Lawrence pictured a man, perhaps Henry, pointing forward beyond a rallying crowd. The man clutches a rifle which directs the eye toward three raised fists, including one which blocks a woman and child from the tip of the gun's spear. Faces of all tonalities with clear eyes directed upward maintain attentive focus amid the chaotic scene of angles and wedges flowing across the composition.

Panel 1, 1955

Collection of Harvey and Harvey-Ann Ross

Panel 2

Massacre in Boston

On the night of March 5, 1770 a squad of British soldiers occupying Boston opened fire on a crowd of colonists. In the painting, the rebellious crowd struggles in the dark chaos of the moment against the redcoats, who are unseen in the composition. Lawrence foregrounded Crispus Attucks, a man of African and Native descent who was the first to die in the conflict. Attucks, who ran from slavery to join the cause to oust the British, is shown here crouching, gripping his chest, and spewing blood, beneath the sheltering arms of his comrades who continue to protest.

Panel 2, 1954

Collection of Harvey and Harvey-Ann Ross

Panel 3

Rally Mohawks! Bring out your axes, and tell King George we'll pay no taxes on his foreign tea... —a song of 1773

This painting's caption comes from the first verse of a protest song sung by the Sons of Liberty, a secret organization fighting British taxation of the colonies. On the night of December 16, 1773, the colonists, disguised as members of the Mohawk Nation, boarded British ships to dump their cargo of tea into the Boston Harbor. Their revolutionary act quickly became known as the Boston Tea Party. Though no fighting actually took place, Lawrence recasts the charade as a violent combat of arms, fists, and axes between masked and unmasked figures. Why? Did Lawrence take the mention of Mohawks in the colonists' song literally? Was he alluding to the struggles of Indigenous people against colonization by the colonists themselves?

Panel 3, 1954

Collection of Harvey and Harvey-Ann Ross

Panel 4

I alarmed almost every house till I got to Lexington.
–Paul Revere

A cloak as black as the steed at the center of the painting camouflages Paul Revere and his clandestine movements. On the night of April 18, 1775, Revere, a Boston silversmith and early revolutionary, barely escaped capture as he rode through enemy lines across eastern Massachusetts to warn every resident he could that the British troops were coming. Revere recalled the events in a 1798 letter from which Lawrence excerpted this title caption. A powerful black horse gallops into the midst of the frenzied scene where several figures strain dramatically as they reach for weapons.

Panel 4, 1954

Private collection

Panel 5

We have no property! We have no wives! No children! We have no city! No country! –petition of many slaves, 1773

Lawrence traced each strike upon the open wounds of these symbolic "men in chains," the phrase he inscribed on the back of the panel. Yet a petition, premised upon nonviolence, provided the basis for the title caption: on January 6, 1773, an enslaved man who identified himself only as "FELIX" petitioned the governor and house of representatives of the Province of Massachusetts Bay for freedom on behalf of enslaved people in the colony. Lawrence excerpted its most urgent plea, which the government heard but did not grant. His image brings to mind what depths of defiance, carnage, blood, and struggle could result from denying peaceful and sound petitions for liberty. In fact, reports of rebellions planned by the enslaved surfaced regularly in the colonies.

Panel 5, 1955

Collection of Harvey and Harvey-Ann Ross

Panel 6

...we mutually pledge to each other our Lives, our Fortunes, and our sacred Honour −4 July 1776

Lawrence honed in on the final words of the Declaration of Independence to envision this solemn pledge as a bounty and a burden for each American to carry in a democracy. A rake and the revolutionary musket cut the composition into two equal halves, creating a wedge around a farmer laboring in 1776. He struggles to bear the burden of his wagonload of hay, a symbol of the nation's bountiful ideals of freedom, which may become a struggle to uphold and defend.

Panel 6, 1955

Collection of Harvey and Harvey-Ann Ross

Panel 7

The summer soldier and the sunshine patriot will, in this crisis, shrink from the service of his country. —Thomas Paine, 1776

Thomas Paine first published these lines in a pamphlet called *The Crisis* during the British siege of New York and incursions into New Jersey. In the wake of setbacks against the British forces, he sensed a wavering commitment in many Americans and urged them to commit to the freedom cause. This painting shows groups of revolutionary soldiers huddled together against the cold in contrast to the single figure at the far right. Seated alone and pensive, he is one of the 9,000 black soldiers who fought within the approximately 200,000 strong continental army and militia. Lawrence drew attention to the solitary struggle of this particular patriot by rendering him in sunshine yellow and positioning his musket firmly upright, signaling his steady devotion.

Panel 7, 1954

The Renee & Chaim Gross Foundation

Panel 8

. . . again the rebels rushed furiously on our men. –a Hessian soldier

The Battle of Bennington on August 16, 1777, was a violent clash between a group of combatants whose backgrounds were diverse in nationality and race. Uniformed Hessian, or German-born, professional soldiers hired by the British army were among the enemy troops that battled against the American "rebel" forces, which included black soldiers, as Lawrence did in this painting. By quoting a letter written on August 31, 1777, by a Hessian soldier, Lawrence used the words of the defeated opponent to testify to the strength of the Americans.

Panel 8, 1954

Collection of Harvey and Harvey-Ann Ross

Panel 9
Defeat

When General George Washington failed to recapture Philadelphia from the British, he led the Continental Army in retreat to Valley Forge, Pennsylvania, in December 1777. Lawrence symbolized the toll of these military setbacks and the tremendous hardships endured by his forces that winter through a visual field of packed snow and ice. The cloaked and bloodied figures in the background face away from us, drawing our attention to the bloody loss of a valuable warhorse in the foreground.

Panel 9, 1954

Private collection

Panel 10

We crossed the River at McKonkey's Ferry 9 miles above Trenton...the night was excessively severe... which the men bore without the least murmur... –Tench Tilghman, 27 December 1776

Lawrence relied on the firsthand observations of General George Washington's aide-de-camp Tench Tilghman to revive the experience of the men who crossed the Delaware River on the night of December 25, 1776, to surprise Hessian forces in Trenton, New Jersey:

> Our party amounted to 2400 Men We crossed the River at McKonkey's Ferry 9 miles above Trenton The Night was excessively severe, both cold and snowey, which the Men bore without the least murmur. We were so much delayed in crossing the river, that we did not reach Trenton till eight OClock, when the division which the General headed in person, attacked the enemy's outpost.

In this painting, he imagined the scene as three small boats crowded with passengers, wrapped in blankets and tossed by choppy winter waters. Rather than highlight the celebrated leadership of the well-known painting *Washington Crossing the Delaware,* Lawrence chose to focus upon the bravery and perseverance of the nameless men who went on to win the battle.

Panel 10, 1954

The Metropolitan Museum of Art, purchase, Lila Acheson Wallace Gift, 2003.414

Panel 11

120.9.14.286.9.33-ton 290.9.27 be at 153.9.28.110.8.19. 255.9.29 evening 178.9.8 —an informer's coded message

American Revolutionary military officer-turned-traitor Benedict Arnold informed the British of General George Washington's movements around New York in 1780 using a numerical substitution system. Loyalist reverend and poet Jonathan Odell received and deciphered the message written in invisible ink: "General Washington will be at King's Ferry Sunday evening next." Lawrence imagined this exchange close up as the informer whispers into the ear of his contact. Who is the rebel? Who is the loyalist? In eliminating the space between the strained faces, Lawrence emphasized the clandestine, dangerous, and sometimes fatal nature of espionage and betrayal.

Panel 11, 1955

Iris and B. Gerald Cantor Center for Visual Arts, Stanford University, gift of
Dr. Herbert Kayden and Family in memory of Dr. Gabrielle H. Reem, 2013.95

Panel 12

And a Woman Mans a Cannon

Margaret Corbin accompanied her cannoneer husband into the Battle of Fort Washington in New York on November 16, 1776. When the British killed him in action, she filled his post by loading and firing the cannon with great accuracy before drawing enemy fire. No taller than the belly of her commander's horse, Corbin struggled against larger forces in battle and for the rest of her life as a woman veteran. In Lawrence's eyes, she is reinvigorated as a commanding figure, standing with her gun upright and in relief at the left margin of the assembled soldiers.

Panel 12, 1955

Collection of Harvey and Harvey-Ann Ross

Panel 13
Victory and Defeat

A wall of twenty-two black cannonballs symbolizes the successful twenty-two-day siege at Yorktown, Virginia, when American troops forced the British occupying the town to surrender, effectively ending the American Revolution. The wall is a backdrop for the sword exchange that took place on October 19, 1781, between two appointed delegates on behalf of Generals George Washington and Charles Cornwallis. Lawrence focused on this imminent transfer of power by creating a gap signified in the white space between the hands—and a pause in the moment of action that seems to hold the new nation's independence in suspense.

Panel 13, 1955

Collection of Harvey and Harvey-Ann Ross

Panel 14

Peace

No Indigenous nations were invited to the negotiations of the Treaty of Paris or consented to the peace accord. The treaty, signed in 1783 by representatives of Great Britain and the United States of America, formally recognized American independence and the new nation's enlarged boundaries. Only a black and white image survives for this painting, which captures the tenuousness of peace through a few daisies growing around three idle cannons. What do you imagine Lawrence's use of color might have been?

Panel 14, 1955

Painting location and inscription unknown

Panel 15

We, the people of the United States, in order to form a more perfect Union, establish justice, insure domestic tranquility... −17 September 1787

The opening words of the preamble to the Constitution of the United States of America focus on the reasons for the founding document's creation: to remain unified, just, and at peace. That vision of tranquility trails off through Lawrence's use of an ellipsis in his title caption, suggesting the four months of intense work in Philadelphia's summer heat by the delegates. Lawrence pictures the 13 state representatives gesticulating and sweating in a complex, oppressive space as if presenting theater on the national stage. A heavy gray and black curtain provides the backdrop to this post-revolutionary drama. Seven sword hilts set upstage symbolize the quorum of states required to define the American people and how they should be represented and governed. This illustrious group agreed that black people would be counted for the census, but not given freedom, citizenship, or the right to vote in what became known as the Three-Fifths Compromise, a concession which ultimately led to the constitution's final ratification. Rather than picture the peaceful moment of resolution depicted in popular images of the signing, Lawrence chose to picture an American creation story defined by moral exhaustion and political struggle.

Panel 15, 1955

Harvard Art Museums/Fogg Museum, Francis H. Burr Memorial Fund,
Richard Norton Fund, Henry George Berg Bequest Fund, Anonymous Fund
in memory of Henry Berg, and Alpheus Hyatt Fund, 1995.23

Panel 16

There are combustibles in every State, which a spark might set fire to.
–Washington, 26 December 1786

Lawrence selected the words for this title caption from a letter written by retired General George Washington to Secretary of War Henry Knox, who was in charge of the federal armory in Springfield, Massachusetts. He expressed concern about mounting social and political unrest there and, less than a month later, in January 1787, Revolutionary War veteran Daniel Shay led a citizen's army of more than a thousand farmers to attack the arsenal.

Panel 16, 1956

Painting location, image, and inscription unknown

Panel 17

I shall hazard much and can possibly gain nothing by the issue of the interview... –Hamilton before his duel with Burr, 18045

The letter written by American statesman Alexander Hamilton before his impending duel with his political rival Vice President Aaron Burr detailed the motivations and regrets for the encounter Lawrence reimagined. Burr's shadow is in the center of the painting. He has just fired the fatal bullet with his extended arm, causing Hamilton's bloody struggle against his needless death. The black and gray coloration of his clothing repeats in the tomb-like structure of cloaks hiding the "field of honor" on the cliffs below Weehawken, New Jersey, on the Hudson River. Hamilton's black top hat rests next to the ominous shadow of his opponent. This stark palette and its associations with death also appear in the background where a symbolic tree of liberty has suffered a severed limb, a mortal gash, similar to the wound in Hamilton's torso.

Panel 17, 1956

Collection of Harvey and Harvey-Ann Ross

Panel 18

In all your intercourse with the natives, treat them in the most friendly and conciliatory manner which their own conduct will admit... —Jefferson to Lewis & Clark, 1803

President Thomas Jefferson wrote a letter on January 18, 1803, giving instructions for the Corps of Discovery expedition led by Captain Meriwether Lewis and Second Lieutenant William Clark. He urged the two Americans to engage in respectful relations with the Native people they would meet throughout their journey. Lawrence chose to depict Lemhi Shoshone translator Sacajawea, robed in red,

in a moment of her own discovery. Here she realizes she is standing face to face, eye to eye, with her brother Shoshone Chief Cameahwait, dressed in blue, and from whom she had long been separated and enslaved since childhood by a warring nation. Lawrence celebrated this tender reunion by forging a heart shape at the center of the composition.

Panel 18, 1956

Collection of Harvey and Harvey-Ann Ross

Panel 19

Thousands of American citizens have been torn from their country and from everything dear to them: they have been dragged on board ships of war of a foreign nation. –Madison, 1 June 1812

During the years leading up to the War of 1812, the British Royal Navy arrested American sailors in international waters and forced them into their service in a practice known as impressment. These activities were a justifiable pretext for war as articulated in President James Madison's request to Congress, which Lawrence excerpted for this panel's title caption. In this painting, Lawrence depicted nameless, faceless American sailors who have been captured and bound. To evoke similarities between the act of enslavement and forcible impressment, Lawrence pictured the men held at bloody sword point and made to march in a stacked procession at the command of the looming British officer.

Panel 19, 1956

Collection of Harvey and Harvey-Ann Ross

Panel 20
Spindles

Spindles are straight wooden spikes used to spin and twist fibers. The cotton gin, invented in 1793, engineered rows of spindles to clean cotton rapidly: fifty pounds of cotton could be cleaned in a single day versus one pound cleaned by hand. Even though the United States abolished the slave trade in 1808, Lawrence knew that the invention of the cotton gin led to the South's maintenance and expansion of slavery as the cotton industry grew to become the nation's most profitable.

Panel 20, 1956

Painting location, image, and inscription unknown

Panel 21

Listen, Father! The Americans have not yet defeated us by land; neither are we sure they have done so by water— we therefore wish to remain here and fight our enemy... –Tecumseh to the British, Tippecanoe, 1811

In this pairing of word and image, Lawrence reflects Shawnee Chief Tecumseh's 1811 loss to the Americans at Tippecanoe (in present-day Indiana) and Tecumseh's resolve to continue to fight against the American military, shown here in blue and white uniforms, for his homelands.

He creates a moment in the painting when Tecumseh's battle had not been lost. The pictorial field, composed largely of densely crossed and reaching arms, depicts the closely matched struggle of would-be occupiers in an already occupied land.

Panel 21, 1956

Collection of Harvey and Harvey-Ann Ross

Panel 22

Trappers

The forceful shapes of two freshly killed Rocky Mountain elk dominate this composition. Their antlers—often used for fighting—contrast sharply against the blue and white snow of the foreground, which Lawrence spotted with fresh red blood dripping from the animals. Around 1812, fur trapping and trading among Salish, Nez Perce, and Euro-American people in the Bitterroot Valley (in present-day Montana) intensified. Lawrence envisioned the strung up prey as an allegory for the land, material resources, and freedoms at stake in the War of 1812 and ultimately ensnared by the expansionist legacies of the conflict.

Panel 22, 1956

Collection of Robert Gober and Donald Moffett

Panel 23

...If we fail, let us fail like men, and expire together in one common struggle... –Henry Clay, 1813

The inscription on the back of this painting identifies its subject as the landmark American naval victory over the British on September 10, 1813, at the Battle of Lake Erie in Ohio. However, the image depicts a scene of utter desolation where a lone American seaman stranded amidst billows of torn sails lays dying. A sword has pierced his eye and blood falls like teardrops while his own weapon slips from his unclenched hand. The clue to this painting's true meaning may be found in its title caption which is excerpted from a speech Senator Henry Clay delivered to Congress to request continued funding for the War with Britain which was going into its second year of fighting. From this text, Lawrence imagined the consequences Clay warned of: the entire nation is threatened when it abandons the common struggle to protect people from their oppressors.

Panel 23, 1956

Collection of Harvey and Harvey-Ann Ross

Panel 24

Of the Senate House, the President's Palace, the barracks, the dockyard... nothing could be seen except heaps of smoking ruins... —a British officer at Washington, 1814

A report written by British military officer George Robert Gleig vividly described the total destruction of the American capital by the British during their invasion. Lawrence imagined the two counterperspectives of this night as a dark trap—a narrow space bounded and lit by firing cannons on one side and by a massive wall of rubble on the other. The only natural element in the painting is the mortally wounded body of a small black and white bird symbolizing the predicament of Washington's civilian population trapped within the city.

Panel 24, 1956

Collection of Harvey and Harvey-Ann Ross

Panel 25

I cannot speak sufficiently in praise of the firmness and deliberation with which my whole line received their approach... –Andrew Jackson, New Orleans, 1815

Against concentrations of red, white, and blue paint, Lawrence laid out the aftermath of General Andrew Jackson's remarkable defeat of the British on January 8, 1915, at the Battle of New Orleans in Louisiana. Jackson credited the resounding victory to the valiant participation of Kentuckians, Creole people, immigrants, and enslaved men who all fought together behind the safety of Line Jackson. The seven-foot-high-wall built by enslaved men out of logs, earth, and cotton bales stretched nearly a mile and protected nearly all the fighters. Lawrence showed us the survivors who lean over to peer at the redcoats they defeated so convincingly.

Panel 25, 1956

Collection of Harvey and Harvey-Ann Ross

Panel 26
Peace

Lawrence's chaotic composition depicts the end of the War of 1812 and alludes to terrible ironies. Some of the Americans who bravely defended New Orleans would remain enslaved after the conflict ended. The United States and United Kingdom had signed The Treaty of Ghent before the battle was fought and the news of the peace accord terms had yet to reach Louisiana.

Panel 26, 1956

Collection of Bill and Holly Marklyn

Panel 27

...for freedom we want and will have, for we have served this cruel land long enuff... —a Georgia slave, 1810

This painting symbolically represents the suppressed revolt planned by Captain James to liberate the enslaved communities between Greene County Georgia and Halifax County, North Carolina, in April 1810. Its title caption comes from a captured letter written by James expressing his unrelenting desire to overthrow bondage and strike out for freedom. The letter read:

> for freedom we want and will have, for we have served this cruel land long enuff, and be as secret conveying your news as

possible, and be sure to send it by some careful hand, and if it happens to be discovered, fail not in the day, for we are full able to conquer by any means – sir, I am your Captain James, living in the state of Georgia in Greene County.

James's emotion is mirrored in Lawrence's painting, which shows the muscular back of a very strong black man reaching up to hold two armed white captors at bay. The life and death struggle embodied in this brutal fight for liberation ruptures the national peace.

Panel 27, 1956

Private collection

Panel 28

Immigrants admitted from all countries: 1820 to 1840 –115,773

A table of immigration statistics published in Richard B. Morris's *Encyclopedia of American History* (1953), one of Lawrence's sources for the *Struggle* series, inspired this now-missing painting. A trio of figures, cloaked in robes, huddles together. The central figure who wears a shoulder shawl clutches what could be a prayer book, a popular possession among nineteenth-century immigrants traveling to America. Lawrence exaggerated the size of the hands to symbolize what it meant to arrive only with what could be carried.

Panel 28, 1956

Painting location and inscription unknown

Panel 29

A cent and a half a mile, a mile and a half an hour.
—slogan of the Erie Canal builders

Who built America? Lawrence chose to credit and showcase the workers who built the Erie Canal across New York state from 1817–25. Three large figures shouldering a canal beam nearly fill the entire composition. Their procession creates a high and stark horizon line that cancels out the view of the sky above them. Lawrence utilized the weight of this line to emphasize the sheer physical power of those who labored under it while underscoring the human capital needed to construct the 363-mile canal system stretching from the Hudson River in Albany to the Niagara River in Buffalo and to fortify the country's pathway to economic and social prosperity.

Panel 29, 1956

Painting location and inscription unknown

Panel 30

Old America seems to be breaking up and moving Westward... –an English immigrant, 1817

Lawrence's final *Struggle* panel takes its subject from a pamphlet written and published by Morris Birkbeck, an English-born Quaker and abolitionist to advertise to his British compatriots accounts from the trail that the promised a fresh start in the American West. In this painting, Lawrence filled the picture plane with the continuous, unrelenting forward movement of covered wagons hauled by oxen over uneven terrain. A conspicuous splash of blood serves as a reminder of those who have sacrificed and died for a new life of freedom. Here Lawrence invites us to pursue the promise of American democracy and to continue to imagine what it means to be on this symbolic wagon and to take up the reins of the struggle.

Panel 30, 1956

Iris and B. Gerald Cantor Center for Visual Arts, Stanford University,
gift of Dr. Herbert Kayden and Family in memory of Dr. Gabrielle H. Reem, 2013.96

CONTRIBUTORS

Sam Ahn

Sam is a senior at Hunter College High School. He enjoys theater and in the future hopes to become an actor, director, writer, or administrator of an Asian American theater company. He is also passionate about sociology and looks forward to exploring careers in academia or public policy.

————

Mya Barnhart

Mya Barnhart is a sixteen-year-old native of Southeast Washington, DC. Since elementary school, she has had a special interest in English and writing. Motivated by her personal struggle with depression, she strives to write elaborate, inclusive, and thought-provoking pieces about social issues and injustices plaguing DC and the world. Now a junior in high school, Mya is enrolled in two AP courses and is the first in her family to be a published author.

————

Lynsey Borges

Lynsey is in the tenth grade at Boston Community Leadership Academy. She lives with her mother and grandmother. What matters to her most in this world is being successful and making her mother proud, because she wants to give back to her for raising her to the best of her abilities and for doing everything for her. In her spare time she likes to listen to music and binge watch TV shows.

Tyler Burston

Tyler Burston, a senior at Friends Seminary, is a writer, artist, actor, and musician. He is interested in the ways that art can be an agent of social justice and a healing practice. His fundamental aim is to craft projects that celebrate and comfort people experiencing marginalization. Tyler will continue his studies at Washington University.

————

Saudia Campbell

Saudia Campbell is a sixteen-year-old living in Southeast Washington, DC. She is a student in eleventh grade at Thurgood Marshall Academy, where she takes part in activism, the dance team, and a sisterhood called HBG. She aspires to be a baker.

————

Trécii Cheeseboro

Trécii is a sixteen-year-old, homeschooled, soon-to-be graduate. Drawing, painting, poetry, and photography have always been of value to her. Trécii aspires to help resolve current issues, concerns, and social problems in her community and globally.

————

Yasmine Chokrane

Yasmine is a sixteen-year-old student attending Stuyvesant High School in New York City. She likes to explore the city in her downtime, walking anywhere she can. She likes to visit local bookstores and museums and has an appreciation for reading, writing, and art history. She also loves hazelnut coffee, scented candles, and garage rock.

Amber Cruz

Amber was born in New York and raised in the Bronx with her parents and two older siblings. Her hobbies include creating art in almost any medium, reading, learning, traveling, and visiting museums. She will attend New York University in Fall 2019 as a freshman with plans to double major in studio art and art history and wants to work as a curator.

————

Zora Danticat

Zora lives in Yonkers, NY, and is sixteen years old. She has a passion for the arts, especially reading and writing. She also loves to sing, in particular jazz and R&B. She is a junior at the NYC Museum School.

————

Kevin Deleon

Kevin Deleon was born and raised in the Bronx, where he and four older half siblings live with their single mother. He is an artist, and drawing has been a part of his life ever since he first saw his sister doing it. He hopes to one day use his animation and sketch work to express his views to the world.

————

Emily Deosaran

Emily is from Trinidad and moved to New York when she was seven years old. Her experience as an immigrant inspired her to pursue creative expression while telling her story. She has never written something based on her life before, so her contribution to this book was very helpful in terms of helping her feel more comfortable in her own skin.

Aminata Dosso

Aminata is sixteen years old. As a junior in high school, she likes to keep herself busy with different activities in the city and by spending time with friends.

————

Jada Epps

Jada Epps is a sixteen-year-old junior at Thurgood Marshall Academy. She enjoys being an activist and effecting change wherever she can. After high school, Jada plans on studying nursing in college and starting her own nonprofit organization for female empowerment. She enjoys eating Reese's Cups while doing homework.

————

Sophie Fishman

Sophie is a sophomore at the High School of American Studies at Lehman College. She was a Spring 2019 intern at The Metropolitan Museum of Art, working in social media. She is interested in photography and is an active member of her debate team and organizes service and activism opportunities for other teens at her synagogue.

————

Rashad Freeman

Rashad is a junior at Newark Academy in Livingston, New Jersey. He lives in Morristown along with his mom, dad, and thirteen-year-old sister. This past school year, Rashad took two advanced placement courses and earned A's and B's in all of his classes. His interests include photography, graphic design, and basketball.

Alyse Gaskins

Alyse Gaskins was born in Norfolk, VA, and raised in Fremont, NC. A sixteen-year-old junior at Thurgood Marshall Academy, she lives in the Fairlawn section of Southeast Washington, DC. She is an honor roll student that enjoys English and Science. Outside of school, she enjoys photography and writing poetry. She plans to attend college and pursue her dream of becoming a professional photographer.

————

Jennifer Hernandez

Jennifer is a senior in high school who attends City College Academy of the Arts. She is interested in cultures from all around the world as well as all kinds of art forms and loves music. She wants to be an architect, animator, and game designer.

————

Amya Hudson

Amya Hudson is a junior at Thurgood Marshall Academy. Originally from Southeast Washington, DC, she loves defying stereotypes. She spends her free time reading, singing, and dancing. As she is strongly opinionated, especially about her culture, she had no problem writing her contribution to this book.

————

Ahmed Iginla

Ahmed is from Brooklyn, NY. He enjoys playing basketball and listening to music. He wants to be an engineer and he likes to break things then figure out how to build them back together. In the next ten years he sees himself owning several businesses and becoming a realtor.

Makayla Jordan

Makayla Jordan is an African American teen writer of prose and poetry. Her writing focuses on the teenage experience and learning how to navigate through a tumultuous and multifaceted lifestyle. Makayla self-published her poetry book, *you*, in December 2019.

————

Braden Kislin

Braden is a sixteen-year-old junior at the Leffell School in Hartsdale, NY. He lives in Larchmont, NY, and enjoys reading, 3D printing, playing tennis and soccer, and hanging out with his grandfather. If Braden isn't doing something amazing he is watching *Game of Thrones* on his couch.

————

Zarina Lewin

Zarina Lewin is a sixteen-year-old who lives in Brooklyn, NY. She joined the Schomburg Teen Curators program because she is very passionate about art from painting and sculptures to writing. She is currently a student at Frederick Douglass Academy.

————

Jamiah Lewis

Jamiah Lewis is a sixteen-year-old African American native of Washington, DC. She is a budding entrepreneur with her own design and fashion business. She also strives to articulate her experiences through literature and art.

Abena Manuh
Abena was born in Accra, Ghana. She is currently a high-school student at the Frederick Douglass Academy. She is interested in modeling and soccer and recently participated in the Teen Curators Program at the Schomburg Center For Research In Black Culture in Harlem. She is also member of the Double Discovery Program at Columbia University.

_____

Makenda Marc
Makenda Marc is a sophomore at Boston Community Leadership Academy. She lives with her parents and three brothers in Hyde Park. What matters to her most in this world is making her family proud because they are the most important thing to her. In her spare time, she likes to meditate and try to understand life.

_____

Munaja Mehzabin
Munaja is fifteen years old and was born and raised in New York. She is a high-school junior. She had the amazing opportunity to work at The Metropolitan Museum of Art in 2019.

_____

Savannah Milton
Savannah is a seventeen-year-old senior at the High School of Fashion Industries. She is passionate about writing, history, and fashion and is looking to pursue a career in these fields. She has recently written two articles for *YCteen* magazine and will be studying in Italy this summer.

Sunah Nash
Sunah is a sixteen-year-old artist from northern New Jersey. She is a senior in high school and has been homeschooled most of her life. Sunah also pursues independent studies in art, writing, the humanities, and the social sciences outside of school. She plans to study psychology and anthropology in college.

_____

Harry Osei-Bonsu
Harry Osei-Bonsu is an aspiring visual artist from the South Bronx who is originally from Ghana. He enjoys photography and drawing and occasionally makes art with film. In Harry's leisure time he enjoys skateboarding, hanging out with friends, and listening to music.

_____

Jillian Peprah-Frimpong
Jillian is a first-generation Ghanaian American student from New York City interested in the way politics influence art and vice versa. When she isn't organizing teen arts programs or studying, she is usually reading articles by fellow teen writers and publishers or napping.

_____

Lindsey Ruiz
Lindsey currently attends the Fashion Institute of Technology in New York City as a freshman majoring in illustration. Her current interests are drawing and painting, in both figurative and realistic ways. She has future plans to become an illustrator, colorist, and cover designer, and to have some ties to the fine art fields of painting and sculpture.

Yoilett Ramos Sanchez

Yoilett is a sophomore at Boston Community Leadership Academy. She lives with her two parents and siblings in Dorchester, MA. What matters to her most in this world is spreading love to others because she believes that in order to receive, you need to give in positive ways. In her spare time she likes to play with her nephews.

————

Brianna Santiago

Brianna is a sophomore at Boston Community Leadership Academy. She lives in Dorchester, MA. What matters to her most is family, respect, independence, and success. For one, family will always be there for you. Respect is something she values because in order to be somebody, you have to earn respect. Lastly, everyone should have their own independence in life, and you don't get anywhere if you're following others around or having them follow you. In her spare time she likes to draw, dance, and sing with her sister.

————

Lucia Santos

Lucia is a sixteen-year-old artist and writer from Seattle, WA. She values her community deeply as well as connecting with the environment and natural world. She was a contributing illustrator for *Rookie* magazine from 2016 to 2018 and is now involved in the Teen Art Group at the Seattle Art Museum.

Kioni Shropshire-Maina

Kioni is a freshman at Loyola Marymount University and has written poetry since high school. Her poem in this book explores personal loss and homecoming as they relate to colonization. She hopes the language allows readers to draw parallels to the losses felt not only by indigenous Americans like Sacajawea, but also by African Americans and other stolen peoples.

————

Lola Simon

Lola is a senior at Fiorello H. LaGuardia High School in New York. She loves to write poetry, prose, and plays and has a passion for painting and the color yellow. She lives in Brooklyn.

————

Madison Stephenson

Madison is seventeen years old and from Harlem, NY. She attends Poly Prep Country Day School in Bay Ridge, Brooklyn. She participated in the Schomburg Center for Research in Black Culture's Junior Scholars program. Some of her hobbies include running track and watching medical TV shows.

————

Yael Torres

Yael is a Chicano teen artist from California. His interests include design, visual and performing arts, and community engagement. He has interned at the Seattle Art Museum and has been an active member of the Teen Arts Group. Yael hopes to pursue a career in the fashion industry as a creative director and fashion editorial stylist.

L'hussen De Kolia Touré

L'hussen De Kolia Touré is a homeschooled high-school junior. He was a 2017 NYC Youth Poet Laureate Ambassador and member of the 2017 Urban Word NYC Slam Team and has served as a Federal Hall Writing Fellow and Word/Works Tumblr Writing and Media Fellow. He has participated in AXE's Find Your Magic Initiative, a movement to celebrate diverse examples of modern masculinity, alongside singer-activist John Legend and poet-activist Carlos Andres Gomez.

_____

Johnná Nicole-Lynn Townes

Johnná has loved writing ever since she was able to form words with a pencil. Sometimes it keeps her up at night and sometimes it helps her fall asleep. She hopes her writings can touch people without making them too sad and overall feel that the best moments come out of understanding as well as hope.

_____

Kori Valentine

Kori Valentine is a student at Thurgood Marshall Academy.

_____

Kylie Vargas

Kylie is a student in the 12th grade at the NYC Museum School. She likes boxing and kickboxing in her free time. She is interested in going into the medical field as well as in anthropology, psychology, and learning more about the history of people of color.

Austen Barron Bailly, formerly The George Putnam Curator of American Art at the Peabody Essex Museum, is Chief Curator at the Crystal Bridges Museum of American Art in Bentonville, Arkansas.

_____

Rebecca Bednarz is Editor for Exhibition Research and Publishing at the Peabody Essex Museum.

_____

Kathy Fredrickson is the Chief of Curatorial Affairs at the Peabody Essex Museum.

_____

Lydia Gordon is Associate Curator of Exhibitions and Research at the Peabody Essex Museum.

_____

Chul R. Kim is Publisher of Six Foot Press and Principal of Charlotte & Company, a consultancy focused on increasing diversity, equity, and inclusion at arts institutions. He is also a Lecturer at the Hasso Plattner Institute of Design at Stanford University. He previously served as Associate Publisher of The Museum of Modern Art, New York, and as Editor in Chief and Director of Publications of the Cooper Hewitt, Smithsonian Design Museum in New York.

_____

Liliana Morales is a Project Manager at Six Foot Press.

_____

Elizabeth Hutton Turner, formerly Senior Curator of The Phillips Collection, is University Professor in the McIntire Department of Art and founding Vice Provost for the Arts at the University of Virginia. She has curated three major Jacob Lawrence exhibitions.

PARTICIPATING INSTITUTIONS

The **Birmingham Museum of Art** houses a diverse collection of more than 27,000 paintings, sculpture, prints, drawings, and decorative arts dating from ancient to modern times. The Museum presents a rich panorama of cultures through its extensive holdings of Asian, European, American, African, Pre-Columbian, and Native American art. Teen BMA is a volunteer group at the Birmingham Museum of Art that gives high-school students opportunities to learn from artists and other arts professionals as well as hands-on volunteer experience.

The **Boston Community Leadership Academy** offers a rigorous college-preparatory program with college acceptance as a graduation requirement. Our pilot school focuses on developing future scholar-leaders through community-service learning and adherence to rigorous academic, social, and civic expectations. Student voices are an integral part of BCLA and inform our school practices and policies. Located in the Hyde Park neighborhood of Boston, BCLA serves a diverse student body with whom we foster empathy, collaboration, and leadership. Its writing program, integrated into the Grade 10 English Language Arts class taught by professor Paula Grillo, encourages writers to think critically, creatively, and independently while interacting with literary analysis, narrative, expository, argumentative, persuasive, and reflective writing tasks. On a daily basis, the students build resilience and stamina, creating a community of writers who reflect on their own work as well as the work of their peers.

Founded in 1870, **The Metropolitan Museum of Art** presents over 5,000 years of art from around the world for everyone to experience and enjoy. Its MetTeens program offers a wide variety of innovative, award-winning programs for teens, who can choose from classes, workshops, and special events designed especially for them. In-depth special summer programs allow young people to tap into their talents and explore The Met collection. Monthly sessions of Art Explore and Saturday Sketching encourage teens to discover works from all over the world and inspire them to make their own art. No matter the skill level of the participants, MetTeens programs are specially designed to develop their skills and connect with art, ideas, and other young people.

Established in 1799 as the East India Marine Society, the **Peabody Essex Museum** is the oldest continuously operating museum in the United States. True to the spirit of its past, PEM is dedicated to creating a museum experience that celebrates art and the world in which it was made. By presenting art and culture in new ways, by linking past and present, and by embracing artistic and cultural achievements worldwide, the museum offers unique opportunities to explore a multilayered and interconnected world of creative expression. PEM's Education Department brings audiences together for transformative experiences of art and culture. Its program values object-focused, social, and multigenerational learning. It seeks opportunities to encourage direct, personal engagement across a variety of media, to introduce and explore the creative process inclusively, and to invite participation in interdisciplinary journeys that foster curiosity and imagination.

The Phillips Collection, America's first museum of modern art, opened to the public in 1921 in Washington's vibrant Dupont Circle neighborhood. It is the steward of an exceptional collection of modern and contemporary art in a dynamic environment for collaboration, innovation, engagement with the world, scholarship, and new forms of public participation. Prism.K12 is The Phillips Collection's framework that supports teachers in creating rigorous arts-integrated lessons and is proven to help teachers of any subject and grade level to craft lessons that deepen student learning. Through a set of six strategies and a suite of online resources, Prism.K12 helps teachers develop rigorous arts-integrated lesson ideas for the classroom. The Phillips has trained thousands of early childhood, elementary, and high-school teachers from across the United States to use Prism.K12 strategies to develop lessons that weave the teaching of art with other core subject areas such as math, science, history, and English language arts.

———

The **Schomburg Center for Research in Black Culture**, a research library of the New York Public Library system, is one of the world's leading cultural institutions devoted to the research, preservation, and exhibition of materials focused on African American, African Diaspora, and African experiences. Its award-winning Education Department provides high-quality learning experiences related to the Schomburg Center's archival collections for students, educators, and people of all ages by building on the long black community tradition of education for liberation. Through the Schomburg's Junior Scholars and Teen Curators programs and activities, young learners can gain new perspectives and acquire skills of inquiry, critical thinking, creative expression, and social action.

———

The **Seattle Art Museum** has been the center for world-class visual arts in the Pacific Northwest since 1933. Founded in 2007, The Seattle Art Museum's Teen Arts Group (TAG) is an intensive program for highly opinionated high school–aged youth who are interested in learning about themselves and the world through art. TAG is designed to cultivate the voice and leadership of diverse young people who share their passion for the power of art to build community. Returning alumnae/i act as

peer mentors for new members as they plan and implement Teen Night Out, meet with artists and creative professionals, and participate in behind-the-scenes experiences and studio-art projects, all designed to make The Seattle Art Museum an inclusive and engaging space for teens.

———

The Studio Museum in Harlem is the nexus for artists of African descent locally, nationally, and internationally and for work that has been inspired and influenced by black culture. It is a site for the dynamic exchange of ideas about art and society. Teen Programs at the Studio Museum provide a safe environment for teens to express themselves creatively. Programs offer students the opportunity to meet and converse with prominent visual artists, express their ideas in discussions, participate in tours and hands-on workshops, and develop important communication and critical thinking skills.

———

Thurgood Marshall Academy is a college-preparatory public charter high school located in Washington, DC's historic Anacostia neighborhood, in Ward 8. Founded in 2001 by law students and their professors at the Georgetown University Law Center, the school upholds U.S. Supreme Court Justice Thurgood Marshall's legacy of equal opportunity through a commitment to provide an excellent education for all students. As a non-selective high school, TMA is open to all DC students and does not enroll students based on academic ability. The average ninth-grade student enters the school with skills three or four grade levels behind. In order to improve their skills and help overcome years of accumulated academic deficits, incoming students receive twice as much English and math instruction (90 minutes of each per day) as they would in a traditional public school. The TMA students whose writings were selected for this book hail from the Advanced Placement U.S. History class, taught by professor Cosby Hunt.

ACKNOWLEDGMENTS

Six Foot Press would like to thank, first and foremost, Kathy Fredrickson, Chief of Curatorial Affairs, and Rebecca Bednarz, Editor for Exhibition Research and Publishing, of the Peabody Essex Museum for their collaboration on this project from conception to publication. We also thank Harvey Ross for his belief and support, including allowing the works in his collection to be reproduced in this book.

The Peabody Essex Museum thanks the generous lenders of the *Struggle* series works, collector Harvey Ross, and curators Elizabeth Hutton Turner of the University of Virginia and Austen Barron Bailly of the Crystal Bridges Museum of American Art. At PEM, we extend our appreciation to Brian P. Kennedy, Lynda Roscoe Hartigan, Kathy Fredrickson, Lydia Gordon, Rebecca Bednarz, Caryn M. Boehm, Bridget Devlin, Claire Blechman, Derek O'Brien, Whitney Van Dyke, Melissa Woods, Caroline Herr, Kathleen Corcoran, Lynne Francis-Lunn, Victor Oliveira, and Jillian Willis for their thoughtful guidance and support.

Six Foot Press is also grateful to Barbara Earl Thomas and the following contributors, participating institutions, and others without whom this project would not have been possible:

The Metropolitan Museum of Art: Randall Griffey, Darcy-Tell Morales, Sylvia Yount

Schomburg Center for Research in Black Culture: M. Scott Johnson, Zenzele Johnson, Brian Jones, Tammi Lawson, Kadiatou Tubman, Kevin Young

The Phillips Collection: Rachel Goldberg, Erica Harper, Dorothy Kosinski, Suzanne Wright

Thurgood Marshall Academy: Cosby Hunt

Boston Community Leadership Academy: Paula Grillo

The Studio Museum in Harlem: Chloe Hayward, Gi Huo, Shanta Lawson

Birmingham Museum of Art: Lindsey Hammel, Emily Hylton, Willow Scott, Rachel White

Seattle Art Museum: Sarah Bloom, Rayna Mathis, Regan Pro

Six Foot: Matt Ballesteros, Josh Maida, Liliana Morales, Sara Rubenson

Bright Sky Publishing: Marla Garcia, Mike Vance

Four Colour Print Group: Paul Reber, Becka Rhoads, Daniel Stamper